101

# A Candle
# for the
# Atlantic

Rosemary Redway

Back row: Huw, Jack and Duff
Front row: Guy and Rosie

# A Candle for the Atlantic

Rosemary Redway

The Book Guild Ltd

First published in Great Britain in 2018 by
The Book Guild Ltd
9 Priory Business Park
Wistow Road, Kibworth
Leicestershire, LE8 0RX
Freephone: 0800 999 2982
www.bookguild.co.uk
Email: info@bookguild.co.uk
Twitter: @bookguild

Typeset in Adobe Garamond Pro

Printed and bound in Great Britain by CPI Group (UK) Ltd, Croydon, CR0 4YY


ISBN 978 1912575 503

British Library Cataloguing in Publication Data.
A catalogue record for this book is available from the British Library.

MIX
Paper from
responsible sources
FSC® C013604

*For Robyn and Alyssa*

# Dedication

I dedicate my book to the memory of my father from whom I inherited my love of the sea and wooden boats.

# Contents

# Author's Note

The following names that appear in my book are pseudonyms:

Duff, Fingers, Bella, Sam.

Despite my endeavours I have been unable to track down Kevin and Sally Gould. Kevin's kindness to us when in Newfoundland was truly wonderful. Thank you.

# Words of Wisdom

Words written in my autograph book by my grandmother in 1947

Four things come not back to man or woman, viz.

The spent arrow,
The past life,
The spoken word,
The neglected opportunity.

It is because I grasped an opportunity that this story came to be written.

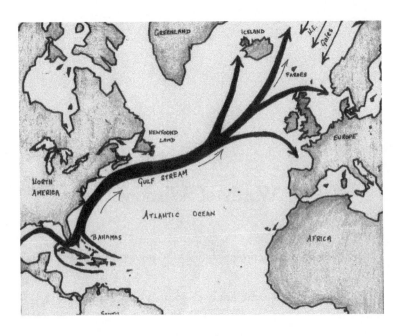

Map of the course of the Gulf Stream

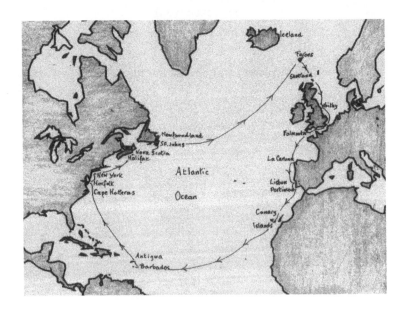

Map of the route of the *Helga Maria*

# Preface

I had the great good fortune, as a child, to have the freedom to roam and explore. Uncle's farm was a meadow away from the bottom of our garden, and I revelled in time spent there amongst the dogs, horses and farm animals. There was always something new to discover, be it a litter of spaniel puppies in the kennels or a beautiful new riding horse in the stables. Two heavy horses worked the land and I remember, so well, the jingle of their harness and the pounding of their hoofs as they ploughed the furrows.

I had the freedom, too, at home, to discover the joy of books. Notable amongst these were those belonging to my grandfather appertaining to medicine, science and polar exploration. Of the latter were the accounts of Nansen's 1893 to 1896 expedition, when he attempted to reach the North Pole in the *"Fram"*, and of Roald Amundsen's expedition in 1911, the very first man to reach the South Pole. Vivid in my mind were the illustrations in those volumes showing the two Norwegian explorers clothed from head to foot in Inuit-styled animal skins in a white and frozen world, with their survival supplies piled high on sleds, and with their teams of huskies. At the age of seven I wanted to be like them and during the harsh winters experienced during the 1940's in the West Riding of Yorkshire where I was born, I loved nothing more than to venture forth in deep snow during a blizzard with my cocker spaniel and little sledge pretending that I was one of them.

At around the age of four years, when on holiday somewhere in Wales with my parents, I had to be dissuaded from climbing any further up a ruined castle tower, eagerly announcing to my mother "this is dangerous, I hope" before she was able to remove me to safety. It seems I was attracted by challenging conditions and anything that seemed like an adventure.

# Introduction

*I hear of a death and promise to write a story*

When I heard that Jack Lammiman, at the age of seventy five, had died, I felt much saddened, but also quite irritated by the fact of his having done so before I'd had a chance, for old times' sake, to catch up with the old sea dog. It was twenty or so years since I had last been in his company and enjoyed the sound of his infectious laughter. There were things I had seriously wanted to say to him. Several times I'd unsuccessfully tried to track him down during my brief visits to Whitby, on England's north-east coast, from my home in Scotland. Ultimately, because of a premonition, I sat on his doorstep, wrote him a letter and posted it through his letterbox. It was a letter of thanks – expressing gratitude for enabling me to have the experience of a lifetime and, as my skipper, for his having brought me, and the crew of which I had been a member, safely back home from a lengthy and challenging sea voyage. I was later comforted to learn that he had read my letter before he died. There was nothing for it, then, but to catch up with him by attending his memorial service at St. Ninian's Church in Whitby and to meet up afterwards at a pub on the quayside which had apparently been his favourite watering hole during his later years.

So it was that on Sunday 19 April 2015 I found myself in the friendly, crowded bar of The Jolly Sailor on Haggersgate and met for the first time Jack's son Peter, very like his father in appearance and with the same down to earth manner. It felt so good to re-establish old acquaintances of twenty years previously when I had lived near Whitby. It made for an emotional afternoon for me and after two halves of the pub's excellent hand drawn bitter (seriously tempted to try a few more) I was becoming embarrassingly tearful. It seemed a good time to leave before I made a complete fool of myself. So finally, after exchanging telephone numbers, email addresses, making promises to keep in touch and last minute hugs, I made my escape – but not before I had promised Jack's two grand-daughters, Robyn and Alyssa, that I would write for them the story, as much of it as I could remember, of the six month voyage I experienced with their grand-dad when I crewed for him in 1992. The girls beseeched me to do it, for, they said, I had known him better than they ever had as a result of my having spent all that time with him at sea.

Back home in the Scottish Borders, re-established into my usual busy regime of dogs, hens, geese and garden, memories of the emotional afternoon spent in the "Jolly Sailor" kept flooding back and, most particularly, the words of Jack's son, Peter – "don't put off till another day what you should be starting, the time is NOW for writing your story." So it was that I began to write notes, as soon as the memories flooded in, on the scraps of paper that I left dotted around the house for that very purpose.

I began to gather everything I could think of that would act as an *aide memoire*. I dug out the scrap book that contained the press coverage that my daughter Sally had collected, and post cards that I'd sent back to the UK from the various ports. I'd used a voice recorder during the voyage and I found the box of cassette tapes, although, disappointingly, I discovered that the sound quality of some of them was poor due to much background noise of wind and crashing seas, and it was a strain to discern what I'd said. It would be a wrestle to extract information from them. But then I remembered that I had kept a journal. For years I have found it a most rewarding occupation to write down my thoughts and observations as I've walked with my dogs in the countryside. I have reams of the stuff in little notebooks – a useful source of articles for the church magazine. Amongst these notebooks on my bedroom shelf I discovered the long-forgotten voyage journal. I was amazed! I couldn't stop reading it – so much was vividly brought back to life for me. Here was the material I needed for my book.

# Foretaste

... the day prior to our departure I delivered my kit, neatly and economically stowed in my sleeping bag, down the companionway to the cabin which was to be my home for the next few months. I chose a top bunk – it had a deck light, or skylight, immediately above, which I liked. I took a deep breath – what I thought could never happen was truly, unbelievably beginning to happen.

What strange chance it was that had brought me to that moment. If life can be likened to a jigsaw puzzle, that moment was an important piece pointing me toward a life-altering experience.

# 1

## A Fresh Start

In 1979 I made the move from my home in the West Riding of Yorkshire, where I was born and raised, to the village of Grosmont, close to Whitby on North Yorkshire's east coast. I was starting afresh and revelling in new-found freedom. I didn't really know anyone and it didn't seem to matter. It was a twelve minute drive from my front door to the beach at Sandsend. My dogs galloped in and out of the breakers and played with seaweed while I soaked up the salt sea air, feeling the wind in my hair as I strode along the strand.

I wandered the streets of Whitby, loving the quaintness, the red tiled roofs of the buildings, the bustling harbour and fish quay, the smells, too, of the sea, of old stone walls, of cooking, of the slightly acrid whiff of chimney smoke. I bought kippers and soused herrings at Billy Fortune's shop up steep Henrietta Street. I explored the ruins of the ancient Abbey and admired the box pews in St. Mary's Church.

A steep winding road led from my front gate up to the vast expanse of the North Yorkshire Moorland that stretched to the horizon; where in August and September the air was fragranced by

1

the purple flowering heather, where I would listen for the chuckle of red grouse or for the clear, piping call of a curlew, and, rarely, catch a glimpse of the twisting, turning flight of a merlin after its prey. The remoteness of those places called me back again and again.

However, it was essential I find myself a job. I spent the summer season as a barmaid in various hostelries and then, as a trained nurse, applied at Whitby Hospital and was most fortunate in securing the post of Staff Nurse in the Casualty Department. I loved my job, the wide range of experience I gained and was proud to be working alongside such an excellent team.

Ten happy, fulfilling years quickly flew but by 1990 a shadow had been cast, for my days had become worryingly haunted, and my peace of mind sabotaged, by a lover from my past who would not leave me alone. I was being stalked, and it felt like a nightmare. Consequently I would often, after work, take the five minute walk down to the harbour-side to watch the world go by, ponder on the confusing vagaries of life and wonder what best to do. One day, while so doing, I suddenly laid eyes on a two-masted schooner where she lay in her berth in the harbour. I was stunned. She was superb, and I tried to absorb every detail of her construction. You couldn't miss her for she stood out from the crowd of modern fishing boats and leisure craft as an authentic antique surpasses the reproduction. Everything about her pleased my eye – the wooden hull and wheelhouse, the old-style deck housing, her planked decks, the brownish-red sails lashed neatly to boom, bowsprit and mainmast. She even smelt good, of sun-warmed canvas and wood, with a hint of engine oil. I noted that at her prow was her name – *Helga Maria*. She reminded me of the model boats my father had made for my brother and me when we were children, one of which, *Patience*, was modelled on a traditional, early 1900's Whitby herring fishing boat, very similar to this vessel lying before me in the harbour.

The Helga Maria in Whitby Harbour
Photo: Sally Tetlow

My father had been in the Merchant Navy during the 1914–1918 war and remained in the service until 1926. He died when I was six years old so I never had the chance to talk to him about the sea, but something must have rubbed off on me for a great deal of my chosen childhood reading was about boats – Arthur Ransome's *Swallows and Amazons* and *We Didn't Mean to Go to Sea*, Erskine Childers' *The Riddle of the Sands* to name but three; I treasured his seaman's knife, his telescope and his mandolin. When I'd moved from West Yorkshire to Whitby in 1979 it had felt like coming home, so good it had felt to be close to the sea, the hustle and bustle of the harbour and the Whitby folk.

I left the quay and headed homeward that day. During the ensuing days, weeks and months I scanned the harbour regularly for sight of the *Helga Maria* and felt keenly disappointed when I couldn't locate her and thought I might never see her again; but I needn't have worried, for one evening, after work, while enjoying well earned refreshment in a local pub with friends, I overheard a snatch of conversation that grabbed my attention. I turned to see who was speaking and was confronted by a short, stocky-built man wearing a navy-blue cable knit sweater. He had a genial, weathered face, with a neatly trimmed greying beard, side whiskers and moustache. He had arrestingly blue eyes with a penetrating gaze. He was puffing calmly on a pipe. I apologised for eavesdropping, explaining that I had heard the words *Helga Maria* and simply had to speak to him about my admiration for the boat. He introduced himself as Jack Lammiman, owner and skipper of the vessel. He had been talking to his friend about the 2,300 mile trip he had made with his boat to Jan Mayen Island, East of Greenland, earlier that year, in 1991. So that was why the boat had been missing from the harbour.

I left them to continue their talk but as I turned away he suggested that the next time I was on the harbour side, as he was going to be living on board for a week or two, to shout "ahoy" and he would invite me aboard and show me round. This was the commencement for me of an amazing acquaintance with both man and boat. I not only went aboard but, a few weeks later, joined Jack and others for a trip up the east coast to Eyemouth, the largest fishing port on the south-east coast of Scotland. I will never forget that experience, my very first sea voyage. I stood in the bow, wind and spray streaming into my face, feeling the rising, falling and plunging of the boat as she competently tackled the waves, hearing the rhythmic chug of her engine, experiencing an exhilaration and sense of freedom which filled me with a joy that satisfied my soul.

I found out a lot more about the boat while chatting with Jack in the wheelhouse. He told me that she was built in the Danish port of Esbjerg in 1929 as a purse seine netter fishing vessel. By 1983, however, she became redundant as a commercial fishing boat and was for sale in Grimsby harbour. He had spotted her and immediately fallen in love with her. On 14 February 1984 he became her new owner and, with friends, sailed her back to Whitby. He subsequently transformed her fish hold into a mess saloon with a table and benches, access to which was gained by a companionway. Leading from the mess were port and starboard cabins, each accommodating four bunks. If extra sleeping accommodation was needed there was the "day bed" in the mess but this was used mainly as a sofa for resting and relaxing. In the forepeak a hatch opened to a second companionway leading down to a small cabin which had been left in its original condition, the four bunks there having wooden sliding doors giving privacy for the occupants. Up on deck, in addition to the original wheelhouse situated aft, Jack had created deck housing mid-ships for a galley, a washroom and the head, or privy. She was an immensely strong vessel, he explained, the Danish shipbuilders being amongst the finest in the world. For the interest of visitors to the boat (Jack regularly took fishing parties out to sea and youth-training runs up the coast) a brochure in the mess read:

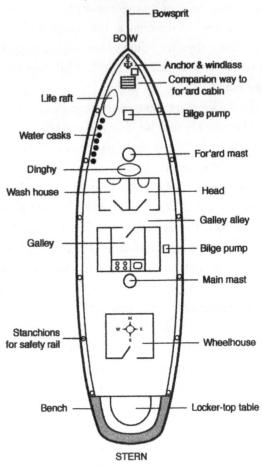

*Deck plan of the Helga Maria*

(drawn from memory)

STERN

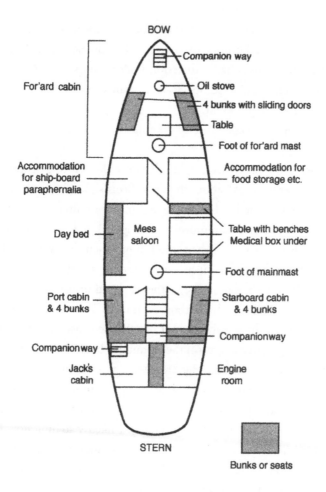

*The Helga Maria - below decks*

(drawn from memory)

BOW

Companion way

For'ard cabin

Oil stove

4 bunks with sliding doors

Table

Foot of for'ard mast

Accommodation
for ship-board
paraphernalia

Accommodation for
food storage etc.

Day bed

Mess
saloon

Table with benches
Medical box under

Foot of mainmast

Port cabin
& 4 bunks

Starboard cabin
& 4 bunks

Companionway

Companionway

Jack's
cabin

Engine
room

STERN

Bunks or seats

"THE HELGA MARIA"

Construction – oak on oak, carvel built.

Length – 65ft. (20 metres)

Beam – 18ft. (5.5 metres)

Draught – 9ft. (3 metres)

Sail area – 1,000 sq. metres

Main Propulsion – 190 HP Hunderstadt Diesel engine.

Navigational Equipment consists of radiotelephone, SBS 500 mile radius, radio direction finder, compass, 2 Radar, Nav. Star, Loran Comp. System, twin echo sounder, full chartroom equipment.

Her engine gives a speed of 7 knots

We stayed on board overnight, the next day visiting Eyemouth museum, where I read about the worst Scottish fishing disaster ever recorded when the local fishing fleet, impatient after weeks of bad weather, awoke to a calm morning and, ignoring the low barometer reading, had just started their line fishing when they were hit by a savage storm. The boats rushed for home but many failed to make it safely back to harbour. They either capsized or were smashed on the Hurkar Rocks at the harbour entrance. Their families on the pier looked on helplessly. A total of 189 men lost their lives that day. Two days after the storm the Eyemouth boat, the *Ariel Gazelle*, limped into the harbour. Her crew were all safe. Instead of trying to make for the shore they'd wisely struck out to sea to ride out the storm. We had time to explore on our own for a few hours but we headed back to Whitby later in the day. I liked watching how Jack was with his boat, there was fluency, a familiarity about the way he nursed her through the sea, like an accomplished rider with his steed. He and the boat were one, born of a long acquaintance.

I was on a "high" when I got home, elated by my brief encounter with boat and sea.

# 2

## I meet Jack's friends. We hear news of the Columbus Venture

During the autumn and winter of 1991, I kept in touch with Jack by joining him and his friends for the Wednesday jazz nights at the Elsinore pub on Flowergate in Whitby, a favourite venue of Jack's at that time. During those evenings I met his long-time friend Edna Whelan, and auburn-haired Lynda Jackson, who, on her own admission, was his "rock" and general factotum. Duff, a dark-haired, bearded Lowland Scot, was there too. I had met him before, when at a concert at the Spa, and questioned him about his name, which I thought unusual. He explained that it was an early Scottish word meaning "dark". The name suited him well. He was working as a semi-permanent crewman for Jack. (It seems to me now that, for whatever the reason, for the better or for the worse of it, there was a quality of inevitability about our meeting and the immediate powerful connection that took place between us. That it was meant to be, as though there had been a form of *recognition*.) On one of the jazz evenings, early in 1992, the subject of interest was not so much the music but rather the forthcoming celebrations

9

to commemorate the discovery by Christopher Columbus of the "New World" in 1492.

Jack had researched the subject and now commenced re-educating those of us who retained only a hazy memory of our history books.

Columbus, he informed us, was a Genoese-born explorer and navigator who possessed the conviction that the world was round, rather than flat. Under the auspices of the Catholic King Ferdinand of Spain, on 3 August 1492, he sailed from Palos de la Frontera in the Huelva province of Andalucia to seek a western passage in order to search for new lands, for spice islands and to spread Christianity. He headed for the Canary Islands initially, to Gran Canaria, and then onwards to San Sebastian de la Gomera where he took on water and provisions for his flagship, the carrack *Santa Maria*, and his two supporting caravels, the *Pinta* and the *Nina*, before sailing into previously uncharted waters. Ten weeks later he came upon the Bahama archipelago, landing on a still unidentified island that he named San Salvador, laying claim to it on behalf of Spain. He found that the region was richly populated by the native peoples. He did not actually set foot upon mainland America.

(Later, looking in my atlas at home, I searched for Palos de le Frontera, a place I had never heard of before. Having located it I then could not understand why Columbus would leave for his great voyage from such an inland location, it being at least ten kilometres upstream from the sea on the river Tinto. However, I discovered that in Columbus' time Palos did indeed have a harbour right on the coast but because of the 1755 earthquake in Lisbon the coastline in that region became altered and Palos instead became the small, sleepy inland village it is today. There is a monastery there where Columbus stayed and a well from which he drew water for his ships. At least seventy sailors from Palos accompanied him on the voyage.)

So, as we sat at our table in the smoky bar of the Elsinore, each with a glass of our chosen liquor, with jazz belting out in the background, we discussed the news that tall sailing ships from nations all around the world were invited to gather in the Portuguese port of Lisbon. They were to be part of a great regatta commencing 24 April 1992 to celebrate the epic voyage of Columbus. On 27 April they would sail from thence in a great flotilla to follow the route Columbus had taken five hundred years previously, subsequently sailing back to their own home ports. For over four years plans had been ongoing for this great event.

We discussed Whitby's rich maritime history, the past importance of its numerous herring fleets, its whaling ships and their captains, notably William Scoresby and his son who were famed for their invention of the "crow's nest", sited at the masthead for lookout purposes, for their navigation skills and their charting of the Arctic coastline while on their whaling trips. There was also the long tradition of shipbuilding, going back to medieval times. In the 18th century three of Captain Cook's ships of exploration had been built in Whitby in Thomas Fishburn's yard – the *Resolution*, the *Endeavour*, and the *Adventure*, while the fourth, the *Discovery*, was built by George and Nathaniel Langbourne in their Whitby yard. All in all, our home port had much to be proud of, and, Jack stressed, it would be regrettable if Whitby were not represented in Lisbon at the great Regatta. His thoughts fell on fertile ground. A Grand Plan began to be born.

# 3

## Plans go ahead for a voyage

The next time I caught up with the group in the Elsinore it was evident that plans were indeed going ahead. Jack estimated that for the *Helga Maria* to make the complete voyage from Whitby, incorporating Lisbon, the Canaries, the Caribbean, then homeward following the Eastern American Seaboard, Nova Scotia, Newfoundland, re-crossing the Atlantic to Shetland and finally back to Whitby, would take approximately four months. Jack decided that with a good supporting crew it was achievable for the *Helga Maria* to attend the Grand Regatta the following spring. His mind was made up. He would go. There was no time to lose. The *Helga Maria* must be readied. That crew must be assembled.

At home I pondered much on that voyage of Columbus and indeed upon the qualities, generally, of the explorers of old. How, in the normal course of events, we nowadays roughly knew where we were going when we set out, but they did not. I felt I understood the spirit of adventure that had so driven them, of their searching beyond the known world.

I thought poignantly of how I would miss the schooner and her crew after she embarked, of what a void it would leave in my life until she returned after all those months of amazing experience. So it was that I felt disappointed, tormented even, to be merely an onlooker to the preparations being made for the *Helga Maria* to follow the route of the intrepid Columbus. I felt as my dog always looked when I left him at home on his own – blighted. But I was pinioned by my demanding job at the hospital. I voiced my feelings to Duff one evening. His response was, "Come with us."

"I would never get leave from work for so long a period."

"Well, you could always ask."

So I did. After all, was not a protracted sea voyage exactly what I needed just then?

***

The Nursing Officer looked up from her rather stunned silence. "Now, I see that you have worked for us now for thirteen years and I do feel that it would be in order for us to grant you leave for the four months you request, and to keep your job open for your return, *if* this is what you *really* intend."

I could hardly believe my good fortune, that she was being so accommodating. I thanked her, said I would confirm details with her, and left the office with my brain swimming – I had a huge amount of planning and organisation ahead of me if Jack would, indeed, take me on as a full working member of his crew. But why would he? My short trip up the coast to Eyemouth barely qualified me for a voyage such as this.

I sought him out the next day and discovered him standing in the bow of his boat talking to an imposing man with a confident, knowledgeable air about him. Atop his clean-shaven, be-spectacled features was perched a faded blue cotton cap that, along with his baggy jumper, appeared to have had a long, hard life. He was introduced to me as Huw Roberts from nearby Sleights, a Welshman and retired Royal Navy diver who had served throughout WW2.

13

He had sailed with Jack many times before, and would be shipping this time as bos'n.

I related to Jack the news that I'd procured leave from the hospital for four months if he would consider taking me on as a crew member for the Columbus voyage. To my delight he said he would welcome me as such and shook my hand. I thought my cup was full until I overheard an aside from Huw to Jack as they were both looking across the deck at me –

"Yon's a flimsy wench," muttered Huw, "she'll not get past Falmouth!"

# 4

## My Preparations

The die was cast. It was up to me now to organise my life and affairs so that I could get away in early April with a clear mind and conscience knowing that I had left things ship-shape behind me at home. I set about making feverishly rapid plans.

**Item one** – my beloved Irish Water Spaniel, Clem. Fortunately I knew a couple who ran a boarding kennels near the Fox and Rabbit Inn on the Pickering road. On enquiry they could accommodate Clem for the duration of my absence and even offered to give him a permanent home in the event of the *Helga Maria* sinking with all lives lost!

**Item two** – my four months' leave would be unpaid. I needed to arrange for income during my absence. The only way was for my house to earn its own living. Through an agency in Scarborough I let my house for holiday visitors and arranged for a girl I knew to clean the house between lets and generally supervise. I fixed for a man in the village to keep the garden tidy.

**Item three** – my little Gloucester canary, my jewel box and a few other items of value I left in the good care of my close friend Stephanie, for their safekeeping.

**Item four** – I managed to sweet-talk my bank manager into allowing me a loan to cover my expenses on the voyage, a sum I would hand to Jack at the commencement of the trip to cover my share of the cost of provisions and incidentals.

**Item five** – Because of my nursing and casualty experience Jack asked me to take on the role of caring for the health and well-being of those on board and so, to that end, I roped in the valuable help of one of the local doctors. Together we filled a big, grey, plastic box with every conceivable remedy for every affliction we could possibly think of, from pills for pain to intravenous fluids for something of a much more serious nature.

I also educated myself by reading a couple of books belonging to Jack, first a medical book dealing with treatments for specific conditions that one might meet when at sea for long periods, and, second, a tome discussing how it was that normally sane and balanced individuals when on land can become detrimentally altered when faced with adverse/dangerous conditions at sea, thereby endangering their own lives, the safety of the boat and fellow crew members. I also dug out from my own bookshelf, to take with me for reading during the voyage, Frances Chichester's *Gipsy Moth Circles the World*, the dust cover of which portrayed the *Gipsy Moth* wallowing in ENORMOUS seas which towered over her, dwarfing her completely. I thought, oh my godfathers, I hope we don't meet conditions like that!

**Item six** – Regarding clothing, I only had a very rough idea of what I might need, but common sense prevailed. I'd seen the four-berth port cabin that I was to share with the other women for the duration of the voyage. Running along the length of my top bunk, joining it to the bulkhead, was a shelf, less than a foot wide, where I could store my gear. We would all share the narrow wardrobe in our cabin which would take a jacket or two. Not a lot of space! I would have to travel light.

Notwithstanding, I visited a store on Church Street where I purchased a pair of white over-the-knee woollen fisherman's socks, a navy-blue reefer jacket and a three-quarter-length black oilskin coat with sou'wester. Kind friends donated a thick white cable knit jersey, a pair of navy thermal trousers (as worn on oil rigs) and a heavy-weight check shirt (as worn on building sites). My daughter Sally loaned me a good quality, thermally lined sleeping bag (which proved to be a boon). From the chemist on Baxtergate I stocked up on multivitamins and cod liver oil capsules (just in case).

… The day prior to departure on the ninth of April 1992, I delivered my kit, neatly and economically stowed in my sleeping bag, down the companionway to the cabin that was to be my home for the next few months. I chose a top bunk – it had a deck light, or sky light, immediately above, which I liked. I took a deep breath – what I had thought could never happen was truly, unbelievably beginning to happen.

# 5

## Departure from Whitby

*"I must say that this is the greatest factor – the way the expedition is equipped – the way every difficulty is foreseen, and precautions taken for meeting or avoiding it"*

The above taken from his book *The South Pole* by Roald Amundsen.

The morning of **Thursday 9 April 1992** dawned fine and clear and the *Helga Maria* was a hive of activity all day while Jack was checking for her readiness to go to sea. Huw and Duff were overlooking the taking on of oil for the engine and water for the main storage tank and for casks and gas cylinders to be lashed for'ard. Huw, in his role as bos'n, was deeply immersed in checking all ropes, blocks, sails, rigging, cables, anchor and windlass and had barely lifted his head from these tasks for many days.

Quantities of assorted gear and boxes of provisions were accumulating on deck waiting to be taken below, so I set to, soon to be joined by Bella, a tall, strong-looking girl with an unruly mane of shoulder-length curly hair. She was twenty six years old and was from the west of England. Between us we made good progress, involving many trips up and down the companionway, stowing stuff in the for'ard cabin and mess to sort out later. Seventy year old Edna Whelan came aboard and she and I went below to our cabin to stow her things and she claimed one of the bottom bunks. The fourth occupant in the "girls'" accommodation would be Lynda who was as usual at Jack's beck and call, seeing to a host of last minute details. She owned a cash-and-carry card and had organised the delivery of the huge tins of meat based meals, vegetables and fruit that cannot be procured at a normal supermarket. Sixteen year old Adrian Magor of Green's Yard, Whitby, was bustling about helping to get things ship-shape. He was seriously seaman-like in appearance, the longer hair on the top of his head severely drawn back into a pony tail, with his side hair shaved away. He was already well used to the sea having spent time with Jack on the boat over several years, and had been keen to accompany him on this voyage. He was obviously at home with the boat – literally "knew the ropes".

Guy Reed, a geologist and environmentalist from Rudston in the Yorkshire Wolds, introduced himself, saying that he would join us later in Falmouth, sailing with us from there as far as New York, where he had work. It was the intention of this tall, good-looking 29 year old to record our progress up to that point with his camera and filming equipment.

The arrival of another crew member was notable in as much as, preparing to come aboard, he slipped and fell heavily on the slimy, seaweed covered steps that ran along the harbour wall, injuring both hands. When he had sufficiently recovered himself he told us that he was a retired steel worker from Middlesbrough. He had read in the newspapers about Jack's 1991 exploits to the Arctic and reckoned he was a man with whom he would be proud to sail, a character and a maverick.

***

(Jack, with a crew of five, had put to sea on 31 July 1991 for a voyage to Jan Mayen Island, just off the eastern tip of Greenland. His mission had been to present a plaque, to be situated on Scoresby Berget, the island's 1,449 foot mountain, in commemoration of the valuable charting of the coastlines of that region in the 18th century by the famous Whitby whaling Captains, William Scoresby, and his son William. In so doing Jack breached a detention order that had been imposed on his boat on 28 June by a Department of Transport official of the Maritime Department from Middlesbrough. Stringent new safety regulations were to be brought into force on 1 July. The hull of the *Helga Maria* was sound, her engine in good order, her mast, rigging and sails likewise, she was equipped with radar and radio, had a regulation life raft and a sufficient number of life belts and life jackets. There was nevertheless a long list of additions and amendments which officialdom required to be carried out. The *Helga Maria* would not be allowed to go beyond three miles out to sea until completion of these. Jack's friends all set to and by 24 July the regulations had all been adhered to. Jack requested another inspection by the D.O.T. Time now was of the essence as the seas around Greenland would start to freeze over and the mission, which he had spent two years planning, would have to be aborted unless he could embark by the end of July. The D.O.T. could give no promise of an inspection any time soon. So, after much deliberation, Jack, normally a law-abiding citizen, was driven to make a big decision. He gathered his crew, announcing that he would sail to the Arctic, alone if necessary, despite the lack of paperwork lifting the detention order. He felt the fact that his ship's bell was apparently two centimetres too small was insufficient reason to be harbour-bound. He knew his boat was safe and the lack of a slip of paper was not going to stop him. Having a low tolerance himself for what he perceived as petty bureaucracy he knew he should leave his crew to decide for themselves whether they would accompany him or not. Down to a man they did, sail they did, evading Customs boats, helicopters, planes and Royal Navy vessels which were alerted to look out for him. Jack completed his mission and the *Helga Maria* returned to a hero's welcome. But he was in big trouble with the D.O.T.)

\*\*\*

At 58 years old, for Fingers, as he became known to us all, this would be his first lengthy time at sea, his only previous experience being of a yachting holiday in the Mediterranean. When I saw the state of his fingers I was convinced some were broken so I suggested to Jack that he was a candidate for the casualty department.

So, at 7 pm, just as dusk was falling, Jack made an executive decision. He chose not to linger in Whitby any longer – it was important to catch that evening's tide. A large, interested and enthusiastic crowd of well wishers had gathered all day on the quayside, watching our preparations, shouting encouragement, asking a million questions. Although we enjoyed and appreciated their interest we were being delayed by it all. As soon as Jack knew that all the crew, and those friends who were to accompany us as far as Falmouth, were now on board, we gathered quietly together on deck as the Rev. Paul Burkitt, vicar of the village of Grosmont, bestowed a blessing upon the *Helga Maria* and those who were to sail in her. As Paul regained the quayside Jack started the engine, ordered the mooring ropes to be slipped, gave a long blast on his horn, slowly cruised his way into the tide and out through the harbour entrance, chased by the echoes of fast fading cheers from the Haven under the Hill, as Whitby is known.

We did not go far. We put into Scarborough a few miles down the coast where we delivered Fingers to the hospital's casualty department. He eventually emerged, broken fingers swathed in bandages, his hands resembling bunches of bananas. Not an auspicious start for him! Meanwhile, free of hindrance, we were continuing our work of readying the *Helga Maria* for the voyage of her life.

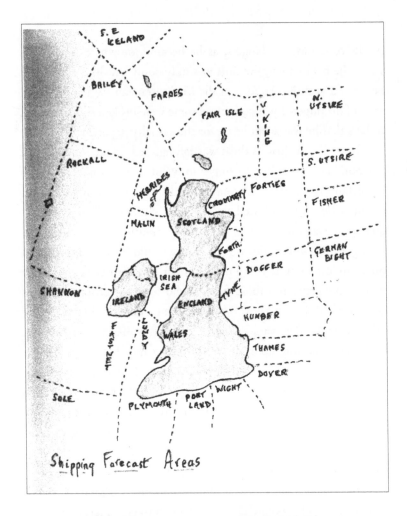

Map of forecast areas around the British Isles.
Taken from my journal.

After this delay Jack really wanted to get on, and although the forecast was not ideal we nevertheless embarked early the following day for Falmouth. Importantly, a strict regime was now established amongst us. Those of us who were totally inexperienced crew would have to learn our roles as deckhands as we went along. We were allotted our watches, our periods of duty on deck. Adrian (Adie), Lynda and I would work alongside First Mate Duff. We were to work the 1200 hours till 1600 hours watch, after which it would be our responsibility to produce the evening meal for us all at 1800 hours. We were then off watch till midnight when we were on watch again till 0400 hours. That gave us eight hours between watches, giving time for sleep or relaxation if we were lucky, although one always had to be prepared for the unexpected. We would stick to this regime throughout almost the entire voyage as this enabled our body clocks to settle to a routine. Each watch consisted of a "trick" at the wheel while observing the course set by Jack, lookout duty in the bow, attending to sail and rope work, meal preparation and generally keeping things ship-shape. Each watch was responsible for producing the next meal, be it breakfast, lunch or tea.

I have nothing written or dictated to record our progress down the east coast, largely, I suppose, because of the high winds, stormy seas and the battering the boat received. For those of us who were completely or relatively inexperienced this was truly a baptism into what the fury of wind and water could fling in one's way. We focused on our duties, heeding Jack's advice in these conditions always to have at least one hand holding on to something and both feet firmly planted for balance. We carried out our appointed watches, snatched meals and slept when we could and throughout it all the *Helga Maria*'s engine chugged reassuringly through a force eight/nine howling gale.

# 6

## Plymouth and Falmouth

A post card to my brother reads:

> "13 April – After two days of heavy battering we've pulled into Plymouth harbour, instead of Falmouth, where we have made all ship-shape again after the storms. We've had showers, not having had our clothes off for several days. There are eight of us aboard, all great people to get along with, I'm so glad to be part of all this. Not due to leave till the w/e due to bad forecast for the Bay of Biscay".

My journal reads:

> "Up at 0600 hours to make scrambled eggs and sausages for Frank and Lynda who are going home this morning on the train."

Lynda and Frank each had a business to run back at home which demanded their attention although Lynda hoped to rejoin us at a later stage of the voyage. Lynda and her husband ran their caravan

24

park at Hawsker, south of Whitby on the coast, while Frank had an antique shop in Whitby itself.

I spent most of the day shifting supplies from the for'ard cabin, where Huw's and Duff's bunks were, into the accommodation, or storage area, which lay between their cabin and the saloon mess. In the evening Fingers treated me to a meal at *The China House*. I ordered baked brill, he had rack of lamb, all washed down with two bottles of wine. We were joined at the bar afterwards by Jack, Bella and Adie.

We remained in Plymouth for several days due to the continuing bad weather of high winds with squalls of rain and snow. From a bonded warehouse Jack obtained more of the large tins of stew, fruit and so on, plus a supply of cigarettes and tobacco. Duff and I also purchased 6lbs sausage, 6lbs bacon, 5lbs stewing beef and 8 pork spare ribs from a local supermarket.

We checked that supplies were in secure places where they would not shift if we were to experience further lively movement of the boat through storms.

After the work was done we were free to make phone calls home, shop or to explore the town as we wished. We later bade farewell to Plymouth on Devon's south coast, watching the red and white striped lighthouse that dominated the headland fade from view as we headed for the Cornish port of Falmouth – Jack's launching ground for tackling the English Channel and the onward route into foreign waters.

We tied up at a rather dilapidated wooden jetty. Returning on my own to the *Helga Maria* after some personal last minute shopping, I was horrified to realise that the tide was well out and the boat was consequently no longer level with the jetty. She was now well below it and the only access to the deck was by a short suspended rope ladder. With some apprehension I started to climb down it but as I did so my weight caused it to swing under the wooden planked jetty and each step took me further under, and away from, the safety of the deck. I was hanging almost upside down, directly over the harbour water, and had no idea what to do. There seemed to be no-one about but I yelled anyway in desperation.

Thankfully Duff had remained aboard and, emerging from the companionway, saw my predicament and instructed me to shift the position of my feet so as to descend via the side of the ladder allowing it to straighten significantly. He then threw up a rope which I managed to attach to one of the rungs of the ladder, enabling him then to pull me closer in. I still had a drop of about six feet between me and the deck. I threw my shopping down and followed it, landing with a jarring thump. After a mug of hot tea in the galley I was able to have a good laugh about my mismanagement of such a simple thing as a rope ladder! I knew I had learned a very useful lesson and had been fortunate not to get a wetting.

Unsurprisingly Falmouth harbour and the rope ladder are indelibly imprinted on my mind!

# 7

## We Leave England

*"Where lies the land to which the ship would go? Far, far ahead, is all her seamen know".*

From an old calendar

Guy had joined us by now and we left Falmouth late that afternoon after tea. Conditions were squally and cold as the fast fading lights of the Cornish coast were lost to view as Jack set the course for crossing the English Channel toward Ushant and the French coast.

The wind increased in strength during the evening and by the time Duff, Adie and I went on watch at midnight the conditions were such as to make the battering we received down the English coast seem like a holiday.

We now encountered severe, huge seas in a force 9 gale and all our tasks about the boat were complicated by having to hold on for support and our legs ached with bracing themselves for balance. The ensuing days continued in a similar way, testing our stamina and demonstrating their violence by hurling Edna from the companionway as she lost her hand-hold when attempting to attain the deck. She sustained painful injuries to her ribs. Guy was

Leaving Falmouth

suffering from sea-sickness and was not fit enough to be on watch, meaning we were now two crew members down, Edna having taken to her bunk with the pain and shock.

Adie was not at all happy with the conditions on board. He disliked his spells of lookout duty in the bow, watching for any hazards that might threaten the boat. He found it hard to tolerate the sense of loneliness he experienced during the solitude of that watch. To feel safe from potentially being washed overboard he roped himself securely, but, thus tethered, was restricted in his ability to move freely about the deck to carry out necessary work. Various things seemed to be "rattling his cage". He announced he would fly home from Lisbon. Bad news – we needed him with all his on-board skills.

His painful hands hampered Fingers in carrying out any tasks. With our reduced crew and adverse conditions it was impossible to adhere to the list, pinned up in the saloon, of the extra maintenance jobs that would be carried out in steadier conditions. Those of us who were fit just got on with the basics.

It was clear that Edna really needed looking after and I necessarily became her full-time nurse. Pain relief was a problem as she could not tolerate analgesics. However, she had her own supply of arnica and was taking that. She had also brought her own supply of Barley Cup, a drink that was kind to her hiatus hernia. Due to feeling sea-sick she was limiting herself to nibbling dry cream crackers. She was most uncomfortable in the cramped confines of her bunk but at least she was safe there. Because of the low head-room of being in a bottom bunk, she was unable to sit up to drink. I gave her fluids via a small teapot, the nearest I could get to a feeding cup, which she could manage to take when semi-lying down. We lashed a bucket securely in her cabin for her to use as there was no way she could make it up on deck to use the head. She was very upset not to be able-bodied but remained amazingly bright and cheerful under the circumstances.

The *Helga Maria* became a casualty herself when her bowsprit snapped under the assault of a particularly daunting wall of water that hurled itself over her bows. Repair would be necessary in the next appropriate port.

The geyser in the galley refused to supply us with any water, hot or otherwise, for cooking, drinks, washing up and so on. We did not need it for personal washing – that was at the bottom of the priority list just then. We had to raid one of the big water casks, securely lashed to the bulwarks for'ard – an added inconvenience in already trying circumstances.

The galley stove was run on bottled gas. It was not set on gimbals, which would have maintained the stove in a horizontal position (as was the compass, set on its binnacle in the wheelhouse) and so, to prevent the cooking pans from skidding onto the deck with each roll of the boat, Bella fixed a "fiddly" – a wire fence device round the top of the stove, effectively retaining and preserving the safety of our next repast. The gas pressure from the cylinder was frustratingly poor, so the meals took a longer time to prepare than should normally have been the case. For personal stability in the galley when preparing meals one wedged one's back against the bulkhead by a foot prised against the oven. To prevent our enamel plates and cutlery careering off the Formica table top in the mess, a "tablecloth" of sail canvas, cut to fit and soaked in sea water, provided an excellent non-slip surface during meal times.

Huw was surprisingly possessive over the galley and liked to take full control when it was his and Bella's turn to cook. He would shut himself in so that she couldn't interfere. Two favourite teas which we enjoyed at this time were black pudding on a heap of buttery mashed potato served with apple sauce, and Spanish omelette. We were always hungry and anticipated all meals with great enthusiasm.

Jack fixed rope rails on both the starboard and port sides which extended from the bow to the stanchions mid-ships where they joined up with already existing safety, or life, rails. This made our movement when working for'ard much safer, where previously there had been nothing to hang on to whatsoever.

Gale force 8

Jack was an unfailingly calm influence within the storm, somehow continuing to puff on his pipe in the teeth of the howling gale. He exuded a reassuring presence. He had experienced this sort of thing before, of course; and so had the engine, and no more comforting sound could there be but of its chugging and rattle rat-a-tat-tat sounds as I was lulled to sleep, warm and dry in my bunk as the boat pitched and rolled.

Jack came up to Bella and me one day and said "You girls are tough and stalwart and I'm proud of you" – a comment we really appreciated. He was gentlemanly and respectful always in his ways towards us, his female crew. Courtesy and old-fashioned good manners mattered a lot to him.

A bonus during the hard conditions just then was that when at the helm we found steering unexpectedly easy.

After tea, most evenings in the mess, Bella would play her flute, to be joined maybe by Fingers on his mouth organ. There was conversation about a myriad of topics and usually much laughter. I would eventually slip away to my bunk to get some kip before going on watch at midnight – drifting into a snooze to the soft sounds of a flute and murmurs of chatter from the saloon.

After forty eight hours we were off Finisterre on the French coast, having left the Channel well behind, and were heading now across the Bay of Biscay toward La Caruna, our next port, in Northern Spain. It became milder, we were in shirt sleeves, and, although we were still in big seas, we had the mainsail up.

My journal states:

"We are tired of hanging onto things, being hurled about, are bruised and have not washed for several days (the latter does not seem to matter a jot). Guy is still sick but attempting to go on watch. The port light has stopped working – must sort that out in La Caruna. Jack is quiet and worried about a cough he has developed which he says is not his usual tobacco cough. He decides to give up his pipe for a while anyway. He is carrying out repair work on the starboard counter which involves much hammering."

**Easter Saturday April 19** – Jack gave me one of his cast-off shirts – sky blue cotton – which he said he had outgrown!
**Easter Sunday** – Guy was improving and feeling well enough to be on watch.
**Easter Monday** – Bella's birthday. We found, and celebrated with, a chocolate Bounty bar. When I went on watch the "Gypsy Kings" were playing on the radio in the wheelhouse, a rousing and cheery sound. To add to the party atmosphere Jack unexpectedly handed me a gin and tonic which came as a delightful surprise. (The set of rules issued at the commencement of our voyage stated that it was to be a "dry" boat when at sea, hence my surprise.)

We had full sail up now and although the sky was still heavily overcast, its gloominess reflected upon the dark grey sea; in contrast I felt Jack's mood was lighter since leaving the worst of the weather behind, for now at any rate.

The atmosphere around Duff, however, was ominous. He was angry that lunch for us was not served on time by the previous watch and refused to eat the soup now brought to the wheelhouse. He clearly resented my access to a gin and tonic! I escaped the discomfort of his presence by going on lookout in the bow. I spent the four hour watch on deck, drenched and exhilarated by still heavy seas. Duff made tea – stew, with fried onions, mashed potato and prunes – delicious.

It was interesting to observe the personalities on board, how people were getting on, or not. Edna, Bella and I, as the three women on board, were getting on fine with one another – no jarring of temperaments. Our skipper, Jack, always in control and balanced, kept an eye on us all – he did not miss much, if anything, of what was going on amongst us. He possessed a composure that hinted at indefatigability. The dreariness of the weather dampened some moods – not mine – my mood was affected by other peoples' moods, which could rub off. There were little frictions cropping up – but more of that later.

Gradually the Atlantic became more considerate to us and as we neared the Spanish coast it was a relief that we did not need to hang on to things so much.

For the notorious Bay of Biscay the weather was being quite kind and we were in shirt sleeves. As we neared La Caruna a port official guided Jack, via the telephone in the wheelhouse, to the designated area for the disembarkation of injured personnel. He spoke fluent English, having relatives in Stroud, Gloucestershire, and was extremely helpful to us in several ways – he aided us in getting Edna to the hospital by car to have her rib injury investigated and advised where to take the broken bowsprit for repair.

Hospital X-ray showed that Edna had two broken ribs but she was reassured that she was fit enough to continue with us at least as far as Lisbon. She was delighted, as this would enable her to see the assembly of tall ships and gather the flavour of the celebrations. Back at our mooring Edna chose to sit in the sun on the quayside while I bought post cards to send home. Having later helped her safely down the narrow harbour steps back on board Edna "refuses to get into her bunk EVER again!" So I prepared the day bed for her in the mess, after which I washed, fell into my bunk and slept for nine hours.

On waking the next morning I discovered that Jack had already set his course for Lisbon and at noon went on watch with Duff and Adie.

From my journal – "In the warm sunshine I am wearing thin cotton trousers and sun glasses. It was good to visit terra firma but so much better to be at sea again. How will I ever settle when I get home? This is such a fantastic way of life."

Jack replaced his sturdy sea boots with wooden clogs and

amused us by executing a skittish jig in them. He wore those clogs in all the warmer climes.

During the watch we saw a skua chasing a swallow which in its fright fell into a bucket of waste water in the galley. Fingers rescued it and most tenderly nursed and dried it. It rested in the mess all day and later took flight.

By this time I had christened Edna "Queen Victoria", for she enjoyed holding court, demanding refreshments and entertaining conversation! What an interesting lady she always was to talk with – an artist and a writer, possessing sound West Yorkshire common-sense and humour. You always knew where you were with her. It was quite a performance, weather permitting, to help her up the companionway, one pushing from behind and the other pulling her up! Once on deck we belted her securely into a deck chair which, in its turn, was lashed to the mainmast. From there she regally surveyed the wide ocean, the Spanish and, as we progressed, the Portuguese coast lines where, set up along some stretches of beach, could be seen row upon row of fish drying on racks in the sun.

# 8

# LISBON and the REGATTA

**Friday 24 April** – At last we were approaching Lisbon harbour. The run-in seemed a long one, the while being guided by instructions coming thick and fast over the wheelhouse phone to lead us to our berth. On our way in we spotted for the first time the splendour of the towering masts of tall ships at their moorings. I felt a great rush of emotion and excitement.

When we were tied up and all made secure we ventured forth onto the quayside and were immediately plunged into the Regatta party atmosphere. Bands were playing and marching up and down. The coloured flags of a multitude of nations billowed in the breeze from a vast assortment of mastheads. Loudspeakers hurled raucous Spanish music toward the crowds. We rubbed shoulders with sightseers and sailors and heard foreign tongues. A postcard to my brother states:

> "*Gran Regatta Colombo* – amazing! Lisbon harbour FULL of tall ships and sailing vessels of all shapes and sizes. Indescribable – a once in a lifetime experience – I'm so lucky and so happy."

Tall ships in Lisbon Harbour

I purchased a navy sweatshirt with the Regatta logo on the front. (Still have it to this day.)

Russian sailors were trying to sell their uniforms – they apparently had not been paid for many weeks. From one of them I bought a handsome leather belt with brass buckle that had an anchor motif on it. (Still have that, too.)

For a couple of days we were able to please ourselves and escaped the hubbub of the harbour by exploring the Lisbon hinterland which was beautiful, wild and, where we were, barely populated. Spring flowers and blooming shrubs abounded.

# 9

## We Follow Columbus

*"The beauty and the mystery of the ships*
*And the magic of the sea."*
From Windjammers by Wm. Gordon and Hugh Lauder

Early on **27 April** we left Lisbon under engine power and hove
to some way out in the Atlantic but still within sight of the
harbour. We waited with steaming hot mugs of tea clasped
between our hands to ward off the chill. Soon our patience
was rewarded, for, glinting in the newly risen sun, one by one
the entire flotilla of tall ships left the port, at first in the faint
distance, but, thrusting their bows into the choppy sea, they
gradually approached, caught up with and finally sailed past us
in their absolute magnificence. The flotilla encompassed every
type and size of craft imaginable – full rigged ships, barques and
barquentines, brigs and brigantines, schooners and all manner of
small craft. High, high up the masts, and along the yard arms,
deck hands tended the sails.

For several hours we watched until the very last one disappeared
into the morning mist. This was what we had waited for, so long,

Deck hands on the yard arms

to witness. It was up to us now to follow, in our own way, time and speed, first to Gran Canaria and then to La Gomera in the Canary Islands.

Jack now hoped for the fresh northerly winds, called the Portuguese Trades, to push us along favourably toward the Canaries. Initially conditions were excellent. However, we began to encounter a heavy Atlantic swell which progressed into a force eight gale. The entry in my journal for **2 May** reads:

"While on midnight watch with Duff, at 1230 hours, I left the wheelhouse for the galley to make mugs of hot coffee for us. Mission accomplished, with two mugs in one hand and steadying myself with the other gripping the rail, I waited for an advantageous roll of the boat so as to swing myself up the steps and into the wheelhouse, when a great wall of water, a freak wave, crashed over the stern. I was ripped from my hand-hold and washed the length of the deck into the forepeak along with buckets and other flotsam. I was soaked, had a bruised shin and cut fingers but apart from being a bit shocked I was fine".

I heard Duff at the helm shout, "Are you there Rosie?" and then, down the speaking tube that connected directly with Jack's cabin below the wheelhouse, he yelled "Jack, man overboard." Jack came rushing up on deck but by that time, amidst the torrent of sea, I could feel the deck beneath me so I knew I was safe and struggled to my feet. I tried to shout but my mouth was full of water. I waded back to the wheelhouse still holding the mugs, but without the coffee in them! I don't think I've ever known anyone so pleased to see me as Duff and Jack were that night.

Sea water had poured into the wheelhouse through the open door, flooded the engine room and Jack's cabin, but luckily no serious harm was done.

Jack gave me a noggin of whisky and I went below to change into

41

dry clothes. Someone gave me a cigarette (I didn't normally smoke but it seemed just what I needed) and Bella gave me a welcome mug of coffee as I went back on watch. The rest of the night was very rough but without further untoward incident.

For several days my Dictaphone was inoperative due to the drenching it had received and I had to borrow Guy's.

Bella had a nasty experience when pulling up the mainsail during the gale – the boom swung over suddenly and she was violently dragged across the deck, painfully bashing both her knees. She commented on how tired she felt afterward, due to the shock and pain.

There was a strong following wind and we were flying along.

I spent some time in the net, taking photographs – totally exhilarating in those conditions. The net, situated beneath the bowsprit, was utilised when we needed access for altering the set of jib or staysail according to prevailing weather conditions. Just a net to separate me from an often angry sea! It was a wonderful place to secrete myself if I wanted to be alone, watching the dolphins crossing and re-crossing the bows as though in a game.

We would often hear their squeaking before we noticed they were there. It always felt a good omen when they accompanied the boat. To lie in the net at the prow like a ship's figurehead, so close to the waves, out of sight from everyone, was, for me, to lose touch for a spell with being human and feel instead part and parcel of the essence of the boat as she plunged and rose through the spume.

We were flying along

Dolphin around the bow

# 10

## Misadventure in Portimao

The boat had suffered injuries due to the latest gales – the radar aerial was broken, there was some damage to the mast and the "Charlie Noble" (a type of cowl for the funnel of the for'ard cabin stove) had blown away. Jack decided to put into Portimao, situated on the southern tip of the Algarve coast of Portugal, for the necessary repairs.

Edna had continued to suffer considerable discomfort from her broken ribs and had to spend much time in her bunk (it being the safest place for her during the wildest weather), and she was still sea-sick. It was decided that she should fly home from here, accompanied by Adie, sad to leave us, but knowing it was for the best.

So, Edna got the support she needed for the journey home and Adie was able to escape home to his beloved Whitby.

Edna's care had taken much of my time so I would be freer now to be more "hands on" on deck. Also now there were fewer mouths to feed, making catering easier too!

After repairs and the airport had been dealt with the *Helga Maria* was anchored just offshore ready to sail the following day, but the

Farewell to Edna

anchor rope became entangled below the water-line necessitating Duff swimming around the bow to fix it. He was revolted by the amount of raw sewage and other detritus floating there – I hoped he would not become ill through accidentally swallowing any of it.

Duff and I had a ghastly misadventure while in Portimao. After tea Jack suggested Duff and I take the grey dinghy ashore for a while, to please ourselves but to make sure to return with a supply of tobacco for his pipe. We dragged the dinghy as well up the beach as we could. It was a steeply sloping beach and it was heavy work. We thoroughly enjoyed having a few hours on our own, but in due course headed back, complete with pipe tobacco and a tin of Golden Virginia for Duff's "home rollies". The dinghy was not to be seen. We scoured the beach but it was, quite definitely, not there. Could someone have stolen it? But the appalling truth began to dawn, that the tide had come up sufficiently to float it away – we had just not pulled it up the beach far enough. There was nothing we could do. It was completely dark by now and the *Helga Maria* too distant for us to attempt attracting attention. The temperature had dropped significantly and we were in thin clothing so we wandered back into the town and walked and walked in order to keep warm. My feet became so sore and bleeding with the trudging that we gave up and decided to camp out on the beach and wait for dawn. I don't ever remember being so cold. My teeth chattered and we were both shivering uncontrollably. We found a sheet of heavy duty plastic and pulled it over ourselves which was probably better than nothing but we had to cling together to conserve a scrap of warmth. The wretchedly miserable night was eventually relieved by the welcome first rays of morning sunlight. We were able to attract attention then by waving our arms and jumping up and down and shouting and were in due course rescued by Guy and Fingers in the dinghy. The latter had floated with the tide to where the *Helga Maria* was anchored, which was a miracle for us all – it would have been very bad news indeed to have lost it. Fingers was furious with Duff, and everyone had been worried about us. I felt utterly stupid and humiliated, but so relieved to be back "home". I never knew if there were any repercussions for Duff, from Jack, about being irresponsible, but it seems to me that we all straight away got together to haul up the anchor, return to normal watches and head off for the Canary Islands.

**6 May** – We were on our way again, the wind had dropped, and the sails hung limply. I made tea, a great corn beef hash with left-over vegetables, pineapple slices with Nestlé milk, finishing with a pot of tea.

I found that getting up each day to a big cooked lunch before going on watch at noon made me feel lethargic during the afternoon. I would help myself to milk and cereals in future. Duff did not eat lunch at all if it was not served on time.

Jack asked me what I felt about personalities on board. He let me know that he was aware of certain frictions. I was well aware of friction between Duff and Fingers, a feud which was concerning and becoming very silly, causing a discordant note in an otherwise harmonious boat. At his best, dark good-looking Duff was wonderful company, intelligent, often very funny, capable, resourceful and the provider of imaginative meals. He was a stickler for things being done correctly, a result, no doubt, of his time in the army and the police force. At his worst he was withdrawn, moody, angry and unreasonable. I didn't work with Fingers at all but he had always seemed easy to get along with and friendly. I didn't say much to Jack, preferring to keep my views private for the moment, but said I would speak to Duff about it, which, later, I did.

Jack also asked me about my feelings regarding a mixed sex crew. I said I had no problems with it, felt absolutely no awkwardness living amongst a group of men. There was enough space for privacy if one desired it and we were all busy, involved in the same work, all of us cogs in the same wheel turning for the common good. I was used to mixed team work anyway through my job at the hospital.

(When asked the same question Huw's only comment apparently was that he felt constrained from showering nude in the mornings!)

Jack invited Bella and me to join him on next year's voyage to the Arctic – we felt pleased to be asked, although I was doubtful that the Nursing Officer would grant me leave again.

We progressed along the Moroccan coast and had sightings of numerous schools of dolphins and the occasional turtle.

**7 May** – Although we were scanning the horizon for sight of land, we saw none. However, several small Moroccan fishing boats came alongside and bartered fish in exchange for six home rolled cigarettes and one dollar! Bella gutted the received gurnard and deep sea bream and Duff and I filleted them and later cooked them for tea, served with potato salad, grated carrot and sweet corn.

# 11

# Gran Canaria – Las Palmas

**8 May** – We finally sighted land which, possibly, might be Tenerife? Jack decided to drop anchor anyway. Gran Canaria, where we were heading, lies between Tenerife and Fuerteventura and there are only thirty or forty mile wide channels between them, hence the questioning which island this actually was! We lunched on beef burgers in Cumberland sauce with mealy pudding and neeps. In the afternoon those who wished swam in the clear, calm sea around the boat and felt wonderfully refreshed and revitalised by the total immersion.

At this point it would seem relevant to describe our washing facilities on board. To the left of the companionway that led down to the mess saloon, and opposite the galley, was a small cubicle, the wash house. There was a tap, which did not work, a sink with a yellow plastic bowl and a small mirror above. The tiny sink was too small for the bowl which sat, consequently, always at a tilt, lessening the amount of water it could contain. When the boat rolled even that small amount of water could end up on our feet. In spite of these challenges, we always took a pride in keeping ourselves spick and span, though never missing an opportunity to swim in the ocean when the conditions were congenial, by either leaping overboard or descending by the rope ladder slung over the side.

Jack despatched Bella, Guy, Fingers and me to take the dinghy ashore in order to purchase lubricating oil for use on the boat, tobacco for his pipe and to confirm our whereabouts. It was latish afternoon when we, in the dinghy, were hurled onto the shingle beach by huge breakers. We dragged it well up the beach for safety. We headed towards sounds of civilisation and lights, and found ourselves in a small fishing settlement. We approached two men, and Guy, who spoke some Spanish, asked where we were. The men, Rafael and Juan, spoke good English, and told us we were in Aquila Plas on Gran Canaria. So far so good, we were on the right island. They directed us to a garage for oil, and then led us to a bar where we obtained Jack's tobacco, where beer flowed liberally and where we enjoyed dancing to noisy Spanish music. We eventually made it back to the *Helga Maria* with our purchases, having had a really lovely time in the company of the locals.

Arriving back on board we were greeted by an incensed Duff who made an awful scene. Huw had to step in to defuse things. This outburst really upset the apple cart and convinced Jack that Duff must go home on the morrow for he was not prepared to tolerate such loss of self control.

This whole episode upset me a great deal, for Duff and I had established a good working rapport. I had a long, long talk with him, to discover the reasons for a continuing intolerance of Fingers, and it boiled down to this:

Duff disliked Fingers talking and laughing with me. He disliked my going ashore with others if Fingers was there. I pointed out to him that when I was off watch I liked to talk to, and generally get to know, the others. I pointed out that I could not do that with him because, when we were off watch, he would shut himself off from me completely, noticeably ignoring me, which was hurtful. I was aware of his reasoning here which was that, before we left Whitby, Jack had apparently made it clear

51

that he did not want "couples" on board. Couples famously cause troubles on a boat, particularly on long voyages. Duff and I had become friends during the weeks prior to our departure, although, in spite of having been strongly drawn to each other, I would not have described us as a couple. However, at Duff's request, we agreed that we would be casual and not display any particular closeness during the voyage. I understood that, but I pointed out that he'd carried things to extremes by shunning me to the extent that he would not even accept from my hand a plate I passed him at tea time, which was unreasonable and unnecessary. Now he was angry to see Fingers taking the time to converse with me, as, naturally, did all the others, something that he would not allow himself to do. I beseeched him to find a way to be more normal in his attitude toward me. I began to see his shoulders relax as he recognised how he had been, and vowed to be different from then on. This last I relayed to Jack who said he would give Duff another chance. I heaved a sigh of great relief.

We now made our way to the harbour of Las Palmas on Gran Canaria. I had become well accustomed now to the great expanse of open sea and sky, the quiet steadiness and simplicity, the rhythm of my life aboard the *Helga Maria*, with time to think clearly in an uncluttered world. I would consequently notice, with a degree of horror, whenever approaching our next port, how demented seemed to be the hectic scurrying of mankind on the land, of wagons and vans and cars whizzing back and forth around the environs of the harbour, the distant people reminding me of frenetically busy ants around their nest. However, we had our own scurrying to do when in port always – for Jack dealt with harbour authorities and organised the taking on of oil for the engine and water for the main tank. Meanwhile provisioning would be carried out at the nearest supermarket and Duff's priority was always to find an available tobacconist so as to stock up on tins of Golden Virginia for his hand rolled cigarettes.

Once moored in the main harbour we saw to the above mentioned tasks, hopefully enough to last us for the four week crossing of the Atlantic toward the Caribbean. Those of us stocking up on fresh provisions from the shops suffered blistered feet from traipsing about in the heat of the overcast, muggy day. While in the port Jack purchased a log for our boat from the captain of one of the tall ships moored nearby. This is a device which, when streamed astern, measures the number of nautical miles covered and which could be checked on a daily basis as a guide to our position.

Once back aboard, being seven days behind schedule due to the storms we had encountered, we wasted no time in setting out for La Gomera, the little Canary Island where Christopher Columbus re-provisioned his ships before finally leaving known territory to search for new lands.

The coastline of Gran Canaria was dramatic with steep rocky cliffs and a backdrop of high mountains. A tall-masted Argentinian vessel, that had been moored near us in Las Palmas harbour, was a magnificent sight as she swept past and overtook us – with her more powerful engine and great spread of sail there was no way we could match her speed.

# 12

## La Gomera in the Canary Islands

We anchored offshore from the port of San Sebastian de La Gomera. There was a great gathering of the tall ships there. Some of us took the dinghy ashore to explore the delightful harbour and quaint township. My enduring memory is of discovering in the town a small chapel where, on entering the dim, cool silence within, a great mural faced us on the opposite wall, graphically portraying the arrival, in 1492, of Christopher Columbus, his ships shown with billowing sails riding on a choppy sea. The painting was clearly of ancient origin. A card I sent to my colleagues in the Casualty Department, dated 12 May, states:

> "This is the most beautiful place. I don't think I will ever bother coming home! A Spanish four-masted barquentine is moored near us. This is where Christopher Columbus took on water and supplies for the *Santa Maria* and his other two ships before sailing off into un-charted seas. We commence our own transatlantic crossing tomorrow".

On **Wednesday 13 May** at 1100 hrs I was writing in my journal:

"La Gomera. Last night after tea we all, with the exception of Huw, went ashore. We partook of glasses of wine in a dimly lit locals' bar that had very thick walls and creaky, uneven floorboards. Later we wandered over to the Plaza where there was a great noisy party for the Spanish sailors whose tall ships from the Regatta were moored nearby. The band played Spanish music all night – fantastic for dancing. We had been soaked on the way over from the *Helga Maria* by a big wave which had swamped the dinghy, so Bella and I had discarded our wet footwear and danced all night in our bare feet. Duff would not join in but instead flippantly 'sold' me to a rather wizened old Spaniard in exchange for cigarettes! The man pretended I was now his woman and was funnily lewd and licentious in his behaviour! But he was horrible to dance with, wrenching my wrists when he twizzled me round. I was thankfully able to lose him in the crowd. It was a wild, unforgettable, wonderful night. Unfortunately, at about 0300 hrs a local lad fell out with Guy and there was a fight. The police took the chap away but he came back later and attacked Duff, hitting him over the right eye with a broken glass. It seemed expedient to leave immediately and we returned to the boat where I stitched the deep gash over Duff's eyebrow straight away to stem the bleeding. There was no need to use local anaesthetic as the amount of beer taken was an adequate alternative! Fingers had also been injured when hurriedly scrambling aboard the dinghy, scraping off a strip of flesh from his shin. I cleaned it, applied gentian violet and loosely protected it with Elastoplast."

# 13

## Our Transatlantic Crossing to the Caribbean

Next morning Duff's eye was very swollen and weeping, he was not feeling well, and, after working on the winch to bring up the anchor as we prepared to leave the island, he crept back to his bunk. Later his eye developed into an absolute shiner and he had difficulty seeing the compass when on our midnight watch.

Around us that night were fourteen fully rigged vessels, looking like ghost ships, for the night sky was clear and the moon cast its silver light on all their sails.

We were rationing our water now. The full barrels of fresh water had to last us till we got to Barbados in approximately one month's time. To be frugal we washed our hair, cleaned our teeth and our clothes in sea water which was hauled up in the red fire bucket suspended on a long rope over the side. If we were under engine power there was hot water available from the outfall but otherwise we faced the hazard of scooping from the sea – as the bucket suddenly filled it almost dragged one over the side. We were surprised to obtain a really good lather with the salt water, our hair did not suffer at all and our clothing was fine, though stiff as a board after being pegged out to blow dry in the wind. It was a joy not to have to iron anything! I liked my crumpled comfortable clothes.

I did a stock-take through the cupboards below so that we knew where we were, food wise. Regarding tea bags, for instance, we had 212 to last 28 days – 9 per day. To be frugal we left the tea bags in the pot and kept topping up with water and fresh lemon slices. It was surprising how long this lasted and how refreshing and good it was in the heat.

A delight now was to eat our meals astern at the locker top which served as a table, enjoying the balmy air for a change, no longer buffeted or blown.

Tea was the main meal when we all met up, with the exception, necessarily, of the two on watch. We were all active and very fit and looked forward to our food with great relish. Often, when we'd finished eating, we would linger a while, relax, and enjoy the feeling of camaraderie and harmony around us. One such evening, as the sun was beginning to set, edging closer to a dramatic, crimson horizon, the vastness of the ocean all around us in its lonely beauty, I experienced, was overwhelmed by, the strangest mood – of feeling lost, emptied, other-worldly, unable to join in the banter any more from around the table. A sort of stillness came over me. Jack noticed that I had changed in some way. He asked me what I missed most of home and all I could think of was "my dog and my kitchen" and I knew he thought I was homesick, but I denied that I was. I knew that that was the last thing I was. The others started to gather the plates and dishes and sensitively drifted away, leaving me alone at the table in my reverie. I sat there a long while. I found it difficult to explain to myself why I should feel this way – it was almost as though I did not belong there. I reasoned with myself that there had been so much that was completely new to me, so much for me to assimilate, over the past weeks. I suddenly felt rather old. I knew that if I had felt like this at home I would have taken the dog for a good long walk and

Dining alfresco

been right as rain when I returned. I could see that Guy needed help hauling up a sail so I went to assist him and pretty soon began to feel more myself. In fact, I suddenly felt so light hearted that everything became hysterically funny. Fingers wandered down the deck toward me, bandy legs spread wide to counteract the motion of the boat and the sight caused me to laugh till I cried! I felt that I had somehow released a heavy load from my shoulders and now felt light as air and joyous. My perspectives had altered. I had undergone a catharsis.

Day followed day now of sun, warm winds, bare feet and shorts. Sleeping bags were brought on deck to air.

We were currently experiencing light trade winds and our heavy canvas sails were unsuitable for those conditions. It was necessary to replace them with lighter weight ones. Consequently, after their morning watch, Huw and, under his tuition, Bella, worked all afternoon adapting a spare sail by putting a tuck in it and making new eyelets. Huw's skills of hand sewing canvas were impressive, as was all his rope work, splicing and so on. (During WW2 one of his tasks as sail-maker aboard one of the ships upon which he had served had been the gruesome task, after other vessels had been torpedoed with grievous loss of life, to stitch the dead bodies into canvas shrouds).

Guy busied himself scraping off old green paint from the wheelhouse roof.

I took on the task of painting our scruffy galley. A lick of white gloss would improve things no end and it was good to have a specific project.

Jack re-introduced me to his book concerning the effects on sailors of being at sea for long periods, the psychological effects and manifestations caused by cramped conditions, food rationing, water shortages, difficulty in maintaining hygiene and so on. Having digested it, now with the altered perspective of some experience, I thought how interesting it would be to observe the dynamics on board the *Helga Maria* during the ensuing weeks and months. We had split up into groups, them and us – inevitable really, as we rubbed shoulders with our watch colleagues and only saw the others in passing much of the time. We were all getting on fine just then, amicably, with no visible frictions.

From my journal I read:

> "Relaxing in the bows, whichever way I look, to the furthest horizon, there is no other boat but our own in this vast expanse of ocean. We are alone out here, yet small birds resembling swallows skim the surface of the waves. A flying fish lands on deck and flaps helplessly about and as I throw it back into the sea Jack shouts that he wanted it for his breakfast! It feels so pure and clean out here, the squalor of land left far behind. Bella is playing her flute and the boat's own music of creaking timbers and clinking of pots and pans in the galley is exemplified by our being fully under sail now, goose-winged to make the most of the following wind. The comparative silence, without the throb-throb of the engine, is uncanny and utterly beautiful".

Jack suggested that Duff and Bella clean the funnel. Duff worked in the engine room and Bella at the top of the funnel. For a couple of hours at least they scraped out black clinker and oily substance, but it took longer than that for the two of them to get cleaned up afterwards! Duff threw his trousers overboard as being past redemption. I had the clean tasks of producing lunch, and later a tea of tinned stew and mash followed by fruit salad with evaporated milk. But the black stuff found its way into everything! After tea I removed the stitches from Duff's eyebrow – well healed now – and cut his hair at his request.

Sailing goose-winged

**Wednesday 27 May** – the clocks were retarded by one hour. Nobody told me and I consequently rose an hour earlier than I need have done at 1000 hrs. I was feeling a degree under as a result of being "scuppered" the previous afternoon as I was helping to haul up the mainsail. Due to a sudden roll of the boat I had lost my footing, still holding onto the halyard, and was flung toward one of the scuppers – both legs shot through and the trap fell down onto my shins. The physical pain was bad, but additionally I realised how ridiculous my predicament was and I felt stupid and incompetent. Someone raised the trap and I extricated myself but not before the sail work was completed by the strong team of Bella, Duff, Huw and Guy. I was able to laugh off the incident but later, after tea, I felt very emotional, went to my bunk and cried, not because of the pain but because I felt so inadequate – too slight of build, too lightweight for some of the heavier work to be a useful crew member. I had been lying there a while with these negative thoughts running through my mind when, to my surprise, Duff sought me out. He was kind and consoling, denied any inadequacy on my part, rather commending me for throwing myself wholeheartedly into all the shipboard tasks. Thanks to him I began to feel a bit better about myself.

One day Jack had a long chat with me, saying he didn't really know me at all, so I told him a few things about myself and my background. Doing so reminded me of the problems I'd left behind me, problems I would have to face in due course on my return, but from which I now felt far removed. Jack was astute and noticed one's moods, demonstrated by his asking pertinent questions. He then went on to muse on the meaning of the voyage we were sharing – the tribute it was to Columbus as a skilful navigator and fearless explorer, but, on the other side of the coin, he was uncomfortable with his knowledge of the horrifyingly dark side of the arrival of Columbus amongst the native populations and the subsequent Spanish colonisation of the islands he discovered. It is a story of immense cruelty, greed, slavery and genocide toward the American Indians. And so we sailed on, but with uneasy feelings regarding what we were representing. This quiet spoken, thoughtful man went on to talk of how much his faith meant to him, of his being a Quaker, of how, when at sea, he felt closer to God, at peace with himself as a free man, able to make his own choices and decisions and stick by them. He attended the Quaker Meeting House in Whitby when at home, liking the silence there and the opportunity for reflection. I was able to glimpse that his quiet faith bestowed upon him a quality not easy to define – as though protective armour guarded an inner knowledge. He certainly possessed a composed personality – on the one hand – but was also a joker and was frequently guilty of uproarious laughter!

From my journal:

"Fingers is rather a dear man, a widower, my devoted friend, kind and considerate. It is so funny when he plays his penny whistle over a cassette tape – the racket is truly awful – but some of the things he plays sound really good. We all join in having pleasant and cosy evenings in the soft lighting of the mess after tea, listening to him tootling.

Huw is a mixture of high spirited fun and garrulousness, the latter always when in the galley, where, red faced and sweating, he battles with the rolling and gyrating of the boat, wedged, prised against the sink with both legs straddled and straining to maintain balance while he prepares lunch. He talks very little of his experiences as a diver in the Royal Navy during WW2. The little he does say indicates a reluctance to discuss events that are clearly still very distressing for him to remember. He is able to recite for our entertainment, from memory and in entirety, the famous poem 'The Green Eye of the Little Yellow God' written by J. Milton Hayes, bringing the tragic story alive with his powerful, lyrical, Welsh voice and the expressive waving of his arms. He is a larger than life character and enjoys an audience. He was born in Anglesey and is vividly descriptive of his childhood there. He is at present busy making sail cloth covers for the winch and funnels".

On the other side of the companionway to the wash house was the "head", the tiny cubicle which accommodated the privy and a toilet roll. There was no real problem so long as one sat quickly on the seat before the lid slammed down and so long as one didn't become unseated as the boat rolled, as was my experience one stormy day when I flew through the door, privy and all, onto the deck, I think unobserved! Unusually large motions could be a problem as the pan's exit dimension was woefully inadequate. Each was responsible for leaving the privy as one would wish to find it. When necessary the privy was emptied over the side by two of the men and when we were well out at sea.

Bella spent a day coating the base of the rubber dinghy with a waterproofing substance and re-adhering puncture mends. She always worked like a navvy, tall, as strong as an ox and was often filthy! She was a smashing girl to get along with. We had a reciprocal arrangement regarding washing our hair in buckets of sea water.

My second haircut on a man was on Fingers one morning and I inflicted a rather effective crew cut. He was pleased with it and said his head felt like velvet.

Journal entry:

"It is 1200hrs. Just had lunch at the locker-top-table aft and it was funny watching Bella balancing to offset the roll of the boat in a heavy swell, hands full of plates and mugs, as she delivered our lunch. Duff and I had to climb over the table today in order to sit down because of lifebelts blocking access on the port side and Jack's tool boxes and paraphernalia on the starboard side. Jack is wearing his tropical cap and, with pipe in mouth, is calmly chucking overboard superfluous items. Round the corner comes

Fingers in shiny blue trainer shorts and khaki baseball cap, skinny arms and legs widely splayed – and the welcome tonic of laughter spills out of me. Our after-lunch mug of tea today tastes of Guy's 'Obsession'. It apparently spilt in a lurch of the boat while he was in the wash house and its aroma has somehow found its way into the teapot".

By **Friday 29 May** we had disappointingly run out of coffee granules, the cocoa tasted mouldy and our tea was too weak to be a satisfying brew.

In the afternoon Jack hove to so that we could swim. This was most welcome as the wheelhouse thermometer had registered 78°F during the afternoon. We wore snorkel kit and were amazed by the numbers of beautiful colourful fish around the hull and keel that we had not been aware were accompanying us. As we swam I felt uneasy about the massive depth of ocean beneath me and of the possible presence of sea creatures that dwell therein and when yellowish brown clumps of Sargasso weed brushed against my body it was a relief to see that that was all it was! Jack positioned himself on lookout up the mainmast to look out for hazards but despite his surveillance Guy had the misfortune to encounter a Portuguese Man of War – its immensely long tentacles wrapping themselves around his neck and shoulders. He disentangled himself and was up the rope ladder and back on deck like greased lightning! It was a thoroughly un-nerving experience, deeply unpleasant for him. I immediately applied the antidote (from Jack's invaluable medical book) – which was to remove any remaining nematocysts with a rough towel, to swill over with sea water the angry red welts where the stings had made contact, and apply soda bicarbonate. However, Guy rapidly developed a malaise so I suggested his bunk was a good idea, together with a couple of pain killers. Several hours later he was feeling distinctly unwell with flu like symptoms and a worrying tightness in his throat and chest. He was relieved of his watches for the time being. Thankfully, by next day, he was well on the mend.

I read up about the Portuguese Man of War, alias Blue Bottle, first, that it was not a jellyfish, as I had thought, but rather an animal made up of a colony of organisms working together. It frequents the warm waters of the world's oceans, drifting on the currents or catching the wind with its purplish-blue gas filled bladder (pneumatophore) sitting above the water, resembling an old warship in full sail. Its tentacles – long, thin tendrils – can extend to 50 metres in length below the surface, although 10 metres is more average. They are covered in venom-filled spikes (nematocysts) used to paralyse and kill fish. For humans the sting is excruciatingly painful, with muscle weakness, breathing difficulty and chest pain as possible effects. They are found sometimes in groups of a thousand or more, and certainly after Guy's incident, we did see them drifting in their hundreds in a bizarre flotilla.

It was **Saturday 30 May** and the temperature in the wheelhouse was 78°F. Bella was exhausted due to not eating much – she was a vegetarian and as we had no cheese left she was ingesting far too little protein for the amount of energy she used.

A pair of Duff's trousers and two of his shirts which had been pegged out to dry had blown away during the early hours – he was most dispirited about this unfortunate loss of clothing and was silent and ominous in appearance with glowering dark eyebrows. During our watch I washed up the lunch things and did two hours at the wheel, while Duff prepared tea, but the wind was spilling out of the sails, the boat veering about and she was hard to manage. Jack relieved me at 0300 hours and changed tack. Guy worked all day on the starboard side bilge pump which was not working and eventually fixed it. For tea we ate boiled beef burgers, mash and baked beans, with Duff's fresh baked scones for afters. As daylight was fading we were yet again treated to a magnificent sunset which Guy filmed, along with sail work being carried out. After tea I would often wander up on deck, leaving behind the pleasant camaraderie in the mess saloon, to seek silence and gaze instead upon the effects of the sinking sun on multi-coloured clouds and rose-tinted sea until darkness fell. In my opinion life could not get much better than that.

We were all having a good working relationship with one another until I noticed a strange alteration in Fingers' attitude towards me which I found hard to understand. It turned out that he was miffed because he had had to hand over the biscuit supply (which he had confiscated and hidden in his cabin, with the intention of throwing it overboard) to Duff, who had now been put in charge of stores.

Instead of a cheery good morning as we passed one another on deck he would turn his head away, completely ignoring me, and this went on day after day. I found it mysterious and a bit irritating. I decided to confront him about it and it turned out that he was accusing Duff and me of guzzling biscuits during our night watch and leaving crumbs all over the chart table in the wheelhouse. He said he discovered them when he went on watch with Jack at 0400 hrs! I assured Fingers that Duff and I almost always had a coffee during our 1200–0400 watch but that we only rarely had a biscuit with it, so the copious crumbs would not be ours. However, the ghastly atmosphere continued and next day Fingers accosted me in the galley, again accusing me of thieving biscuits, that he didn't want to speak to me again and thought it disgraceful that in such a small community we would stoop so low as to nick biscuits. Clearly, the man had gone potty!

By **3 June** things were going from bad to worse and Fingers informed me that everyone on board knew how bad I'd been in nicking biscuits! The situation depressed me in spite of myself but I just had to try to ignore it all. It was so silly and futile. I dared not tell Duff what he'd been saying or there would have been trouble.

The thermometer in the wheelhouse showed that it was 82°F in the wheelhouse, with high humidity. Despite the heat I decided to re-varnish the bulkhead over the chart table, a job made harder due to the exaggerated rolling of the boat. I helped Duff make chapatis for tea. I noted that there was very little bread mix left.

Jack was in the Bosn's Chair up the mast carrying out maintenance work.

Our supply of tea finally ran out and joined the coffee as a fond but distant memory. We were compelled to resort to a tin of dandelion coffee which we discovered when rummaging in the accommodation, seemingly a left-over of Edna's – it was not *too* bad to drink.

The bilge pumps were requiring approximately 1,000 pumps per watch, and we were sharing this task between us.

**Thursday 4 June** – "I've had a chat with Jack about the Biscuit War. He says that Fingers told him that the whole Columbus adventure had been ruined for him by biscuit crumbs! I feel better for my talk with Jack. He had told Fingers not to be so petty and to go forward and sort things out with himself. I feel relieved now to know of Jack's feelings on all of this. He is aware of the atmosphere that has been created throughout the boat by Fingers' strange paranoia".

The heat and humidity, the monotonous rolling of the boat, food rationing, shortage of gas, worry about the possibility of hurricanes and typhoons (since we were approaching the locality and season for them), vagueness regarding our position due to Jack's relying on dead reckoning only, were all contributing to a state of mind, apparently common amongst sailors confined on long voyages, which Jack called "the channels". A situation soon set to rights as soon as land is sighted and a beer in the offing! The "Raynav", our electric navigation system, did not work when we were under sail as it was the engine which generated our electricity.

Duff had been extremely well behaved and restrained during the Biscuit War but seemed tired and was clearly looking forward to setting foot on land and downing a few pints. He was being generous with his cigarettes to Bella and had given a pair of shorts to Huw whose own shorts had blown away. As a natural comedian his sense of humour was a joy – a real tonic – and so were Huw's stories at tea times which had us all laughing. Huw had fallen several times on deck and was sleeping so much that Jack ticked him off and told him he was not fit to go on the Arctic voyage in August next year.

On **June 5** it continued to be hot and humid – 82°F – making it an effort cleaning the galley and producing a tea at 1800 hours of beef stew, peas and Smash. Fingers was still not speaking to me but ate the tea I made and took to him in the wheelhouse. This was the first meal he had accepted for several days with which I had been involved, so perhaps he was beginning to come round at last.

Surrounding the boat next morning were flocks of Manx shearwaters skimming the waves in their graceful flight, hardly flapping their long, narrow wings, the tips sometimes actually shearing the sea. They were identifiable by the darkness of their upper parts, and as they wheeled, by their white chin, throat and under parts. The high rounded crown of the head and the down-turned tip of the beak gave the bird a most distinctive appearance. These elemental birds have a reputation for longevity and also for covering vast migratory distances across the Atlantic in their apparently effortless gliding flight. They live out there in the great ocean wilderness only seeking land during the breeding season. It was a joy to have their company for a while.

However, while on watch during the afternoon I had felt "blue" for some reason and had not been concentrating well at the wheel. We were sailing very close to the wind when suddenly the compass shot over from 310° to 230° – I had lost the wind from the sails and Jack had to get up from his rest and with Duff and Bella took down the sails and I was able then to correct our course. I vented my anger with myself afterwards by pumping the bilge 600 times!

Jack hoped to reach Barbados on the morrow, or the day after, in order to let us stretch our legs and find a pub if we felt like it, but, most importantly, to re-provision with tea, coffee and fruit at the very least. Our next stop would then be Antigua and onwards up the east coast of America.

We were all much quieter, and tired, and I did feel more easily irritated by little things – like Guy leaving an awful cooking mess in the galley when he had prepared lunch and the way he left flying fish in a saucepan stinking to high heaven! The Biscuit Rat Bag could get on one's nerves, too, if one let him. I wondered what my irritating habits were to the others.

**Sunday 7 June** – I was up in good time and washed myself in sea water ALL over and felt refreshed. Duff was silent and serious on our watch – he had run out of cigarettes. Fingers gave me a pack of Camel cigarettes for him but Duff refused to accept them. Nice gesture of Fingers' though. There was a heavy swell and steering was a swine. Jack changed tack at 1600 hours. Hearing hurricane warnings on the radio made us feel a bit edgy. Fingers was beginning to talk to me a little and the tense atmosphere was relaxing slightly. When off watch I was reading the book by Robin Knox Johnson, *The Columbus Venture*, which I found to be an interesting and appropriate read.

In my journal I note that:

> "Tori Amos is singing on Bella's radio, Guy's mattress is airing on deck and he is lying on it, reading, looking well bronzed. Bella, like me, is writing while we sit in the bow".

It was some time later, when the hue and cry had all died down, that Huw and Bella ruefully owned up to me that they were the ones guilty of the biscuit crumbs on the chart table, for they admitted to scoffing biscuits liberally during *their* late watch! They had enjoyed observing the ensuing rumpus.

**Monday 8 June** brought rough seas and a sudden squall during middle watch while I was at the helm, and, the second time it had happened to me, the wind took the sails aback. Jack and Duff had to take the sails down and reset them, this at 0300 hours. For me, the worst feeling I had on board was inadequacy, either because I was not strong enough or because I did not fully comprehend. The sail work had bewildered me initially but my own drawings of the rigging had clarified things for me greatly. If only it were organised so that each person had a specific job to do when there was a change of tack it would be so much better than all hands on deck rushing about and getting in everyone else's way. "Wherever I go I get crushed in the rush so hang back and feel stupid".

By **Tuesday 9 June** I was getting rather fed up with the smokers' cravings for nicotine. Duff had collected a bag full of fag ends, fiddled about endlessly separating the tobacco from the filters and then smoked the result in his pipe. The smell was awful.

On **Wednesday 10 June** at 1300 hours there was a queried land sighting by Jack, and again at 0400 hours, verified by him at dawn. Long before we could clearly see the land we were amazed to hear the tones of steel band music wafting toward us – what an exotic, festive sound that was! So, BARBADOS AT LAST after 28 days at sea crossing the Atlantic – it felt, to me, quite an achievement. Also, it had been mostly done in the way of the seamen of old, by dead reckoning and a skipper's instinct for the sea.

# 14

## Our Caribbean Experience in Barbados

We moored at the quayside in Bridgetown, Barbados. After we tied up, Fingers and I, and later Duff, eagerly went ashore. We needed to find a bank, a few beers and, importantly, to soak up the atmosphere of the town. The milling throngs of the local people seemed the happiest I had ever encountered. We watched them go about their business in the hot, sunny, colourful streets while we enjoyed a few beers in a nearby bar to the accompaniment of calypso music and general hubbub.

Back aboard the *Helga Maria* the tasks of taking on oil and water were going ahead as normal. An American couple, enjoying their wedding anniversary and looking for some fun, chatted to us from the quayside – they needed no second invitation and excitedly joined us aboard, bringing with them their plentiful supply of champagne. We had a most pleasant afternoon in their company! Jack however was experiencing delays regarding our passport inspections, and the delays carried on into late evening, goodness knows why. (Jack had taken charge of all our passports at the commencement of the voyage and these he had to produce of course at every foreign port we visited.) Duff remained on board to deal with these issues while the rest of us, Guy, Fingers, Huw, Bella, Jack and I set out to explore the town. I thought Duff would be a bit miserable at being left behind so after a while I returned to keep him company. This turned out to be a stupid waste of time because he did not want my company due to his not having any cigarettes and consequently being in a diabolical mood. He had bought a packet of twenty in the afternoon, off Fingers' credit card, but it seemed these had already been smoked. (Total insolvency and nicotine addiction are not good bed mates but these had haunted Duff all the time I had known him and seemed part of his dark and partly hidden background.)

The rest of our crew returned to the boat at 0300 hours, very merry.

The next morning I felt irritated that Duff had been such an unsociable curmudgeon the previous night and just ignored him and got on with my own business. I bought a cassette tape of calypso music at the duty free shop, and phoned my daughter Sally to let her know that all was well. (Sally was my appointed link with home and I contacted her whenever we put into port.) I bought, wrote and posted cards to those at home who would be waiting for news and, before returning to the boat, purchased two packets of cigarettes for Duff. I did a bit of "straight talking" to him when I handed them over!

The afternoon was spent re-provisioning for the boat at the big, colourful supermarket with its trestles burgeoning with a great variety of fruits and vegetables, many of them unfamiliar to us.

Duff and I prepared a tea of Caribbean chicken with sweet potatoes. We all went to "Pinks Place" afterwards, which was a locals' bar, for beers, and then to "The Ship Inn", a sophisticated little night spot, to listen to amazing music and watch some very sexy dancing! I got us in by cashing a traveller's cheque. It all got too much for Jack and Duff and they slouched off, leaving the rest of us to enjoy ourselves. It was a wonderful night and we got back at 0330 hours.

At 0900 hours on **Friday 12 June** we left Barbados in a rain squall, listening to steel band music on our radio with the throb of the engine as a background. It was sad to leave such a lovely place but it was so good to be back at sea again. It always was. Just as we were about to slip our mooring ropes a young Barbadian called Michael brought us gifts of mangoes, coconuts and plantains – he generously refused any remuneration.

**Saturday 13 June** brought an overcast day turning soon to torrential rain as we passed Martinique to starboard, a very green island but mostly enveloped in cloud and mist. During my lookout on middle watch the sky continued to empty itself onto our patch of sea and Bella, grabbing a golden opportunity, joined me in the bow and we both stripped off our clothes and luxuriated in God's own shower, rinsing away the salt from hair, faces and bodies and felt totally refreshed.

Later a squall hit us and the boat was rocking, rolling, pitching and tossing. Spectacular lightning jaggedly splintered the whole sky. All sails were taken down apart from the mainsail.

I made a tea, at Jack's request, of fried potatoes, beans, eggs and corned beef and it was good to see him tucking in so eagerly to the sort of meal to which he'd decided he had a fancy. In fact we all tucked in eagerly. On a longish voyage, with different people cooking the various meals, perhaps not all of the people could be pleased all of the time. I always had such a good appetite that, with only a few rare exceptions, I enjoyed everything that was put before me. One of the rare exceptions was of my own blunder – to conserve the fresh water in our casks I tried cooking the vegetables in sea water. It was a disastrous failure and created an inedible meal. What I should have done was to dilute the sea water with the fresh.

Jack had seemed rather tetchy with Huw and Duff recently,

telling Huw he was too old and that Duff was not fit enough, that his heart was not strong and that he did not re-provision adequately. Guy thought Jack delegated a great deal and was too quick to condemn others when he was far from infallible himself, for example, Jack's vague navigation around the Canaries, there being no operative generator, poor tools, little in the way of alternative navigation aids (the sextant being left behind in Whitby), his time assessments being way out for reaching destinations. That he forgot what he had told certain people to do, which caused confusion when two people went to do the same thing. My own gut feeling, at that time, was that I had faith in Jack's long experience of, and instinct for, the sea, and his intimate knowledge of his boat and its capabilities. Anyway, Jack appeared immune to any implied criticisms.

On **Sunday 14 June** we passed Guadeloupe on our port side. At 1900 hours we were streaming past Montserrat on our port bow, Antigua was dead ahead. There had been a fire in the engine room at 0900 hours apparently! I never heard what had caused it – fortunately there was only minimal damage.

The sole of Fingers' left foot had become infected through a small cut. I cleaned it, dressed it and, as there was considerable inflammation and swelling, put him on antibiotics.

Duff made a delicious tea including plantain (a new fruit to us, looking like an oversized banana), capsicum, sweet potato, pumpkin and onion.

Bella played her flute for us after tea as a farewell gesture – it was to be her last night with us, as, if she could get a cheap flight from Antigua, her intention was to fly home on the morrow for family reasons. She wanted to rejoin us ultimately so as to complete the voyage, but was not clear when she would get a return flight. However, she requested that Jack wait for her in Antigua.

# 15

## Our Caribbean Experience in Antigua and a threatened mutiny

*"Let every commander keep before him this eternal truth, that to be well obeyed he must be perfectly esteemed."*

The "Old Man" from an old calendar

The *Helga Maria* stood off Antigua till it became light on the morning of **Monday 15 June** and then secured a mooring in St. John's harbour. Our boat was completely dwarfed by a huge cruise liner which berthed closely astern of us and started disgorging its passengers onto the quay, a seemingly endless stream of amply proportioned holiday makers. I could not help making the comparison between our bronzed, honed crew and them. I felt no envy for their luxurious life style.

Some of us went ashore to have a look round. Beyond the immediate working area of the quay was an attractive, air-conditioned modern mall with expensive looking shops displaying luxury items. But these temptations were not for Duff and me – on walking straight through and emerging on the other side, we stepped off the "platform", as it were, on which the mall was built, into another world altogether – a hustling, bustling, crowded world of the local inhabitants, shanty dwellings of cardboard or scrap wood, corrugated iron shacks, sheds, shops, narrow, cluttered streets, dark men smoking goodness-knows-what in dim recesses. One certainly picked up the true flavour of the island when wandering in that zone. We were fascinated.

Guy had flown back to England to attend the wedding of his brother, but would return the next day.

Next morning after breakfast Jack suggested that to be in Antigua and not take a trip to Shirley Heights would be a waste of an excellent opportunity. Accordingly, a taxi was ordered mid-morning to take us there. I had heard of the place but had no knowledge of its significance.

We were adopted by Curly, a friendly Antiguan taxi driver, who offered to take us wherever we wanted. He drove us to the southernmost tip of the island, depositing us at the bottom of a steep incline where a stony, dusty track led us up to the top of the hill. There were some local women there selling strings of coloured beads and I bought blue and green necklaces which I wore for the rest of the voyage.

On reaching the summit we were astounded by the breathtaking, unforgettable prospect that met our eyes. We were overlooking English Harbour from a height of 150 metres above sea level. Around us were the weathered ruins of a military complex, which, we read from the information board, was built in the late 18th century, had been used as a signal station and was named after General Shirley, the then Governor of the Leeward Islands. Antigua was a prosperous and commercially important sugar producing island at that time, as were the other Caribbean islands. They had been developed by the British Colonies, and Antigua was known as the "Gateway to the Caribbean". Colonial efforts were made to ensure its safety from invasion. We studied a plan of the complex as it was then, which included a guard house, magazine, kitchen, officers' quarters, adjoining parade ground, a forty bed hospital, canteen and a cemetery. An obelisk commemorated the officers and men of the 54th Regiment (2nd Battalion Dorsets) who had died in service in the West Indies between 1840 and 1851.

Furthermore, we learned that Horatio Nelson had arrived in Antigua in 1783 as Head of the Squadron of the Leeward Islands. His role there had been to develop the British naval facilities at English Harbour and to enforce stringent commercial shipping laws. He remained there till 1787. He built Nelson's Dockyard, an impressive asset for the island and had a house there but preferred to live on his ship in cramped conditions rather than dwell in vermin infested premises! He apparently was miserable throughout his entire time in Antigua. Serving under Nelson at that time was the future King William IV during whose reign Britain abolished slavery in the Empire, giving native Antiguans immediate and full emancipation.

The earliest European contact, although he never landed there, was made by Christopher Columbus on his second Caribbean voyage in 1493. He named the island Santa Maria la Antigua (after the miracle-working saint of Seville). It was not until 1632 that finally a settlement was made there by a group of Englishmen from St. Kitts.

Curly the taxi driver, seeing us as an opportunity, let it be known that Runaway Beach was a great place for recreation, so the next day Fingers, Duff and I hired him to take us there. On arrival we discovered a dream of silver sand, turquoise sea and palm trees, the whole beach entirely to ourselves apart from a man serving behind a little kiosk bar sheltered from the sun under a thatched canopy. It was so perfect I had to pinch myself to believe that this was real!

We ordered some beers, found deck chairs and spent a leisurely day, ordering cheese and ham sandwiches when hungry. The downside was being eaten alive by insects! I wandered off a little on my own and could not resist the temptation to swim naked in the warm sea hoping to rid myself of the pesky blighters for a while. Duff joined me, which upset Fingers who was now not speaking to me again.

Duff explained that he would like to live and work out there. I knew that he had much unhappy "history" back at home and it would, admittedly, be a way for him to leave that all behind, but what about me? I didn't want to lose him.

Plantain, an alternative type of banana, was cooked for breakfast next morning along with bacon and tomatoes – a very tasty combination of flavours.

> "Jack and Huw both find the heat here exhausting. Jack is tired and variable in mood. He is waiting to hear from Bella regarding when/if she can rejoin us, but he is impatient to get away from here as the longer we are in port the more he has to pay the Customs Men. He cannot fully trust the locals and worries that he is being fleeced. Also we are twelve days overdue and the threat of hurricane and typhoon hangs over us".

We met the skipper of a hovercraft that had earlier entered the harbour and tied up close by. *La Viginga*, as she was called, was an enormous, gleaming-white ultimate example of a modern vessel. He invited us to have a trip out to sea in her.

This was an incredibly exhilarating experience, the initial acceleration alone leaving one literally breathless with our skin stretched taut on our faces. Its top speed was around 47 knots and at that speed rode well out of the water, driving us below decks for safety's sake. We were led from the bridge to the galley where coffee was served, and we sat for a while in the smart, air-conditioned lounge, a sophistication we thoroughly enjoyed. The craft was able to cross the Atlantic in 48 hours compared to our 29 days!

Aboard *La Viginga*

The high speed trip had totally refreshed us but we ultimately had to return to the smelly harbour with the unspeakable filth floating about in the water.

In the afternoon of **Friday 19 June** Duff and I went to Runaway Beach again, this time taking Huw with us. Duff was very quiet. Huw was full of hell because of Jack's rudeness and hurt to him and was threatening to fly home – he was fed up with the boat, the heat, the discomfort of his bunk and the state of the galley, which, try as one would, greatly lacked anything approaching what would normally be looked upon as acceptable hygienic conditions in a hot climate – too many nicks for crumbs and particles to collect. There were flies everywhere in Antigua, plus midges, mosquitoes and ants. Back aboard, after tea, we sat together in deck chairs for'ard and as night fell we were lethargic in the heat and idly watched legions of harbour cockroaches, some of which attempted to join us by marching along our mooring ropes! We summoned up sufficient energy to dissuade them and thankfully we saw no rats! I bought insect repellent to spray in cabins and galley.

Duff told me how depressed and hurt he was by Jack's dismissive attitude toward him – he felt he was rarely acknowledged by him. Duff, unlike the rest of us, was supposedly a paid member of the crew as First Mate, but had not been receiving any remuneration. This had put Duff in the unenviable position of having to borrow money from us – a totally unsatisfactory situation.

Meanwhile Jack was in an unusually low mood, had become uncommunicative and was frequently inconsistent. He had progressively shown great favouritism of Bella, had made her his protégée, and had certainly seemed badly down since she flew back to England (financed largely by Huw). Her popularity with Jack was understandable. She had so comprehensively endeavoured to become cognisant with every nuance of the working of the *Helga Maria* that she had perforce been beside him a great deal, "learning the ropes", which had pleased him and they had become very close.

What with one thing and another I was having a great sense of apprehension regarding the morale generally of our crew which could not have been much lower – I found it hard to envisage how the rest of the voyage would go.

Jack designated me as cook on day work for the rest of our time at sea. I went off to do some provisioning on my own, a local boy helping me back to the boat with the supermarket trolley. I later cooked a tea of turkey wings with hot pepper and a dash of pepper sauce, mixed vegetables and potatoes.

On Saturday a three-masted schooner entered the harbour and berthed aft of us. Duff found the opportunity to speak with her captain who ultimately offered Duff a job on her as a deck hand. It was very tempting for him – it would mean regular pay, work all week and back to port at the weekends. It was a dilemma for him, to be divided between his loyalty and his word to Jack and his strong desire to settle and work here in Antigua. This would be such an easy way for him to make a new start. I sat with Duff a lot and let him talk about what he wanted to do with his life. He would certainly like to live and work out there. Where was all this going to end? I went to bed about 11pm after popping out to buy cigarettes for him and a glass of wine for myself.

On Sunday Duff was not at all well, with headache, aching bones, vomiting and diarrhoea. I barred him from the galley. The rest of us were all right.

Guy returned at 1pm, and although he was tired after the wedding and the travelling, he and I commissioned Curly to take us to Hawksbill Beach, a private beach belonging to a smart hotel, renowned for its coral reef and multitudes of glorious coloured fish. We were able to hire goggles and flippers and, swimming out, were soon transported into the magic, tranquil world of the reef. I lost track of time as in wonderment I swam amongst a myriad of fish. I never thought I would do anything like this – what a marvellous experience it was.

The author at Hawksbill Beach

The hotel lay within beautiful parkland planted with unusual trees, one of which was labelled "Turpentine Tree" from which is sourced turpentine from its resinous sap. Amongst the Tamarisk and coconut palm plantation holiday chalets were dotted about and, interestingly, an old sugar cane crushing mill. The beach was named after a rock, just offshore, the profile of which resembled a hawk's beak.

Duff was feeling better by the time we returned, drinking tea and eating bread and butter. There had been no more vomiting but he had slight diarrhoea and he felt weak. I was not altogether surprised to hear that Fingers had decided to fly home that afternoon. I was sad that I had not been there to wish him goodbye.

Huw had a rash under his chin – cause unknown, treatment nil.

Jack wouldn't come to the beach but I spent some time in his company as he seemed to want to talk about human relationships and what he felt were his failings with them. He said that he had voluntarily cut himself off from his grandchildren because he did not want to fail with them as he felt he had with his own children.

He was taking little or no notice of Duff but was being a little less cruel to Huw.

Huw had spoken on the phone to his wife, Lil, during the day, which had been a comfort to him in one way but had made him miss her even more, if that were possible – clearly a most devoted couple, he spoke to me often about her, and so warmly. As Huw said, "Man misses woman when away at sea, but that leaves a lot to look forward to and is all the better for the waiting".

In my journal I wrote:

"There are two little dogs that live in the environs of the harbour. The brown and white bitch appears to be in whelp. Her mate is brown all over and all the island's dogs look very much the same. These two look contented enough and apparently get fed with scraps. In the market, though, I had spotted a sad specimen with aggressively short, clipped ears. It was scratching dementedly, presumably covered in fleas or suffering from mange, poor thing. There is apparently a high mortality rate amongst pups – they starve to death. An interesting sight has been of a pelican that lives in the harbour and has food thrown to it by the locals. Frigate birds fly overhead, and bright green, agile little lizards scuttle about the walls. Insects abound, driving us below decks to the mess for our meals".

On the opposite side of the harbour there was a casino and a very nice restaurant, "The Hemmingway", after Ernest, where Huw and I had an excellent meal one day. Huw purchased a floppy-brimmed straw hat that day as protection from the sun, for he had become burnt and was not tolerating the heat well.

Duff and I went for a stroll together in the evening and found a little locals' bar with a good atmosphere and music. We later returned to the boat for coffee and chat – a happy friendly evening.

It was **Monday 22 June** and we received the news that Bella was unable to rejoin us in Antigua. Consequently there was no further need for remaining in St John's. Jack was restless to get away from Antigua immediately. I decided that I must do some straight talking to him regarding the low morale and dissatisfaction which had been manifest on board for quite some weeks. We were on the verge of a mutiny. As captain of the *Helga Maria* Jack was, of course, in ultimate command and was responsible for the seaworthiness, the safety, navigation, and, importantly, the crew management of our vessel. So, to represent us all, I went privately to him and cited the following complaints:

a.  His favouritism of Bella – too marked and causing resentments.
b.  His dismissive attitude toward First Mate Duff and lack of acknowledgement of his comments and ideas. (First Mate Duff's wish to instigate life jacket and emergency dinghy practice for instance.) Telling him he is not fit enough.

c.  His rudeness and aggression to Huw – too old, too sleepy, too deaf etc.

d.  The poor maintenance of equipment. Alternative navigation aids zero – no sextant – and existing RayNav (Loran) system was not operative. No log for counting the number of nautical miles achieved. (The log was lost in heavy seas and not replaced.) The generator was not operative.

e.  His hurtful comments to Guy (who as an intelligent, modern young man had made observations and suggestions which had been dismissed out of hand).

f.  His borrowing money from us.

As I expected there was no comment from Jack, but at least he knew the score. He appeared oblivious to the criticism, remaining obdurate. He knew his own mind and said he needed no-one. Basically he was intimating that if there was a mutiny, he would carry on regardless, without us.

I accompanied him on a last minute supermarket shop. Returning to the boat I discovered that Duff had packed a bag and was threatening to leave unless Jack would speak with him to guarantee support and allow him to feel valued. Jack said nothing but started the engine and began to pull away from the quay and there was a terrible moment when I thought that Duff would make a leap for it and I didn't know what to do. But the gap between the boat and the quayside widened very quickly and the moment was gone and only by a whisker was Duff saved from being left in Antigua without a bean in his pocket or his passport.

# 16

## Heading toward the east coastline of North America

We left Antigua at 0200 hours and it was an enormous relief to me to be back at sea, with, thankfully, all of us aboard and a mutiny averted. It was a mercy to leave behind the harbour smells, the town's drains, the multitudes of insects, the humidity and the heat that Jack and Huw, particularly, had found so trying. I felt sympathy for Horatio Nelson who had had to tolerate it for several years without our modern benefits of insect repellents.

**Tuesday 23 June** was a very hot day with a good wind allowing us to be under full sail of jib, foresail, stay sail and mainsail. Sadly an atmosphere of gloom existed on board. Duff was going through "cold turkey", and barely eating at all. He looked pale and ill. Why oh why, I asked myself, do people seek to destroy themselves with nicotine, drink or whatever?

Guy was making the best of things by getting on with cleaning the galley stove. He dismantled it completely and spread the parts on the deck in the sun, scraping off quantities of greasy residue and finally wire-brushing all the parts before re-instating. A very thorough job he made of it, as he did with any task he undertook. The stove worked more efficiently as a result of his efforts.

Middle watch on **Wednesday 24 June** was grim, Duff not communicating with me at all, discharging me of my duties and sending me below at 0200 hours! He cooked and ate porridge for his breakfast but would take nothing from my hand. What on earth was I supposed to have done wrong? What a saga of catastrophes with him since we left Whitby:

a.  Stiff-necked and stubborn and ignoring me when we started out
b.  Cross-purposes with Fingers
c.  Cross-purposes with Jack
d.  Cross-purposes with Guy
e.  Fight and cut eyebrow
f.  Frequent episodes of withdrawal symptoms from nicotine creating a bad aura all around him
g.  Depression
h.  Episodes of ill health
i.  Cross-purposes again with me.

Jack, Guy and I agreed that the atmosphere on board was thoroughly bad. Jack was determined that Duff would never sail with him again. My own morale was good enough but I was saddened by Huw's dejection, Guy's quietness, Duff's withdrawal.

Guy netted some Sargasso weed that was floating around the hull, and, putting it in a bucket of sea water, was able to examine it closely. It was full of small crabs and many other creatures and what looked like fish eggs – a veritable mini universe of life.

I busied myself by painting along the starboard gunwales all afternoon in the grilling sun and afterward made macaroni cheese and tossed salad for tea.

By **Thursday 25 June** Duff's diarrhoea had returned and was now green! I instigated preventative measures, hoping to avoid any spread of this to the rest of us. I fixed up a bucket of strong disinfectant hand wash outside the head and gave orders that EVERYONE, WITHOUT FAIL, wash their hands in it after they had been in there. Duff was very rude and refused to take any advice regarding treatment for his condition, for instance, what was suitable to eat.

The next day he was a little better and had some return of appetite. He borrowed tobacco from Jack, smoked it in his own pipe and felt somewhat cheered.

> "The sea is very blue, the sun is hot and the breeze is fresh – excellent conditions to meander IF we did not have a schedule to keep, an ill man on board, we were not short of milk, if Jack was not short of tobacco, if First Mate Duff was not out of tobacco, if we were not low on drinking water".

By the following day my patient was most unwell – feeling dreadful, feverish, with headache, looking ill, drawn and thin. I was worried about him and was wracking my brain to know what best to do. It would have been good to have had a doctor on the end of a telephone line. My only alternative to that luxury was to take out the medical book and look up **"Oral Rehydration for Acute Diarrhoea"** and write it into my journal:

8ozs. Fruit juice (rich in potassium)
½ tps. Honey or corn syrup (glucose essential for absorption)
A pinch of table salt
8ozs. Boiled or carbonated water
¼ tps. Baking soda

There were other similar variations on the same theme.

**Causes of Diarrhoea:**
Gastro-enteritis
Cholera
Amoebic or bacillary dysentery (shigellosis)
Viral enteritis
Salmonella
Staphylococcal food poisoning
Typhoid
Paratyphoid

This was a terrifying list, and I had no idea what organism I was dealing with.

Suitable antibiotics were listed for all of the above conditions – and I didn't have any of them in my medical box! My only course of action, as far as I could see, was to soothe his gut with *Asilone* ( similar to *Milk of Magnesia*) before food and at bedtime, to give fluid replacement and to nourish him with bland foods, particularly plain boiled rice, plain white bread, cream crackers and to encourage the drinking of clear fluids and avoidance of milk. I considered *Imodium* tablets to terminate the diarrhoea but decided whatever the bug was it was best to let it run its course naturally. Duff said he would not have taken medication anyway. He was thin, pale, hollow eyed, a physical and mental wreck.

Huw developed a rash covering most of his body. He cleaned his bunk, sprayed it well and had a good all-over wash himself. There were still insects on board from Antigua and I spotted a cockroach in the galley which Guy was hunting down.

Life was an endurance test just then. Jack bemoaned how the balance of the crew was all to pot and how it only needed one person to create a general bad atmosphere.

Duff refused to have me on watch with him during middle watch but I stayed anyway and spent most of my time on lookout.

"Middle watch – 0100 hours – I spent an hour at the wheel and am now on lookout. It is a velvet night with a sky so crowded full of stars I know I have never before seen the like. There is little wind and we have only staysail and mainsail in use. Lying back in the bow, watching how, with the gentle rolling of the boat, the mast swayed to and fro across that amazing firmament, with a shooting star occasionally streaking silently away, I am lost in the pure magic of this tropical night."

One of my self-appointed tasks on these night watches was, for the sake of hygiene, to boil all tea towels and dish cloths, after which I would pump the bilge 500 times.

I know Duff did not stick to his diet wholly, if at all (I received reports of his having chucked his rice overboard), but he did continue with the *Asilone* and after a couple of days his symptoms began to settle, commencing a more normal eating regime, much to my immense relief.

I discussed nicotine addiction with Duff so that I could try better to understand what he was going through. He could only say that he felt desperately low all the time. It was so sad to witness the waste of the "golden hour" by such a craving, to witness his misery and the disappearance of his true personality. And yet, did I not have a longing of my own, which was for him?

Guy had a cold and was drinking honey and lemon.

On **Friday 3 July** the middle watch produced a thunder and lightning storm with torrential rain.

Duff was now covered in spots. An unusual skin condition consisting of vesicular eruptions which burst, followed by peeling of the skin. I hoped the vesicular fluid was not highly infectious! I wondered if this was in any way connected to his recent illness.

I made kedgeree for tea, which I fancied, and which I thought would make a nice change, but the men seemed to prefer their meat and two veg.

"I feel in an aggressive, sparring, but surprisingly cheerful frame of mind. Guy has engineered in the wash house nearly all day attempting to make the tap work. Having failed, he has abandoned the enterprise, leaving my newly glossed paintwork scuffed with black, oily hand marks everywhere. I am b------- if I'm going to clean it up".

The boat's radio had now gone "kaput" – this was serious for us as it meant that we were incommunicado with the outside world without the ability to send out a May Day call or to receive a weather forecast.

I noted that the water in the big casks had algae on it, so all drinking water would have to be boiled so as to be on the safe side.

**Saturday 4 July** – Way ahead of us, in America, it was Independence Day. Sadly there was heavy rain and wind in New York where the tall ships were to put on a display. However, there was little or no wind where we were, only slow progress being made – we could have walked faster. We had a three course tea to celebrate the day, of tinned salmon, chicken supreme, sponge cake and tinned peaches.

The boat rolled from side to side, side to side, as, after tea, I sanded down the port gunwales prior to varnishing.

Guy went out in the dinghy and captured a Portuguese Man of War, which he now had in a bucket on deck, had christened Fred, and was interestedly observing its behaviour. Initially it was frightened and contracted, but then it relaxed, the incredibly long tentacles exploring the confines of its prison. Later Guy released it back to the sea, a generous and forgiving gesture, I thought, toward a species with which he had, earlier, had such an unpleasant encounter!

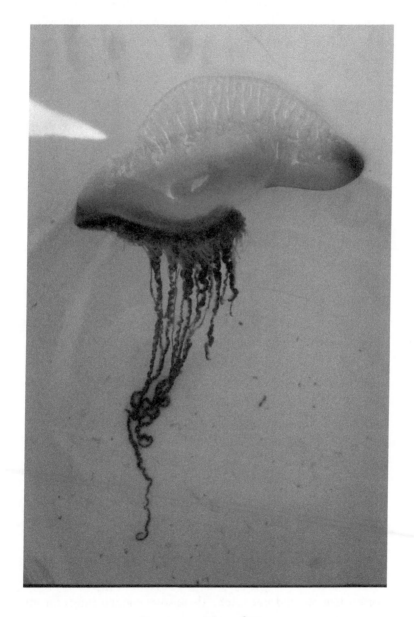

Portuguese Man of War

We were steering a westerly course toward the east coast of the United States of America. There had been a twenty-foot tidal wave on that coast the day before. We were experiencing very little wind where we were, making one to two knots at the most. Middle watch was marked by:

a. The accidental loss and drowning of Duff's duvet over the side.
b. The construction of a sun top by me, for me, out of a bunk curtain. Not a great success as it needed elastic, which I did not have, rather than the twine that I did have.

The sails were all now down due to lack of wind and the engine started. Jack looked concerned about things and was agitatedly marching up and down the deck, with, I believe, typhoons on his mind.

Duff was manic because of lack of nicotine although I knew he was trying to hide it.

Guy and I had a swim before tea and found we had hard work to keep alongside the boat against a strong swell which was sweeping us away from the bow. Hungry after the exercise we demolished a grand tea of beef stew, green beans and macaroni, after which Duff's craving for a cigarette was so great that I suggested he climb the mainmast to the crow's nest as an exercise to divert his mind. Shortly he called down to me that now was a good opportunity for me to watch the sunset from there.

So, after his descent, for the first time I ventured up the mast to what was our wide-range lookout. The crow's nest was an oaken barrel, secured to the main mast by steel hoops, the base of which was a trap door for access. Without the encouragement of Duff, and particularly the guidance of Guy, I doubt I would have made it, for the ladder which gave access to it, for a not-particularly-tall person like me, did not reach. There were enough rungs for my feet but I ran out of rungs near the top for hand-hold and I was all for coming down again. Guy shouted up that I must not, and that

The Crow's Nest

I *could* do it, and that I must let go altogether and reach up my arms to push open the trap door, and then, by resting the back of my head against the base rim of the barrel, walk up with my feet and ease my way in, letting the trap door drop down again so that I had a good floor to stand on.

From that point on it was plain sailing, but I shall never forget those moments at the top of the swaying mast when I had to let go and have faith. But WOW! It was fully worth it, for the vision I then received of the great orb of the sinking sun as it gradually dipped beneath the horizon, so widely displaying its gold, its roseate hues, finally its deep crimson over the vastness of the ocean was truly awe inspiring and unforgettable. I was filled with the strongest sense and appreciation of the glory of Creation. I fully understood how it was that Jack felt closer to God when at sea, experiencing a brand of beauty, purity and peace hard to find elsewhere. I descended, eventually, in a contemplative frame of mind.

Afterward, as we sat in deck chairs for'ard, I chatted quietly with Jack, Guy and Duff, bare feet on the still-warm deck, the peace of a moonlit, starlit, tropical night embracing us, phosphorescence weirdly glimmering around the hull and stretching away from us like a magic carpet, as Huw, at the helm, attended to our course.

On **Monday 6 July** I awoke to a very brisk morning with a goodly swell and white capped waves. All sails were in use, plus the engine, and we were doing about 7 knots.

> "Huw is exasperating – I put the kettle on for a hot drink before I went on middle watch and while I quickly washed my face he filled the kettle with cold water so I had to make do with a cold drink instead. ALSO, disappointingly, the sweet biscuits that Duff made yesterday for our coffee breaks have ALL been consumed – not one left for him and me!"

The wind became gale force with rough seas and rain squalls. Stormy weather in more ways than one – I made the mistake of pulling on the jib sail halyard before Duff had finished re-threading the sheet to the whisker pole – he went through me like a dose of salts. His fury took me aback! He certainly did not suffer fools gladly and I was obviously now on his list of fools. Tea was curry with garlic bread and chapatis, but Duff would not partake of it, for, when earlier he had thrown down his cap in his anger at me, it had blown away, along with his appetite!

I spent a miserable middle watch with Duff – not one word in conversation uttered throughout. It was flat calm, hot and hazy, with a temperature of 84°F – a contrast from yesterday, necessitating engine power again.

Sargasso weed lay in mustard-coloured trails across the sea. Flying fish, sometimes singly, sometimes in dozens, shot out of the sea like arrows and with their outstretched wings sailed on the wind for amazing distances across the surface of the water. Many landed on deck and Jack enjoyed eating them.

Guy was not in a good mood because Jack had been ribbing him about his desire to know EXACTLY where we were all the time:

"When you get home, my lad, BRIDLINGTON will be written up clearly and you'll know where you are and all the streets will be named if you look up for the signs."

Huw appeared to be VERY deaf, and sick of things.

Duff – I did not stay near him long enough to find out what mood he was in. Jack and I together removed sacks of rubbish from the galley and stored them in a crate which was now securely lashed for'ard for disposal when next in port. We swilled the galley well with a view to ridding ourselves of the curse of any remaining insects.

A launch tore past, bristling with fishing rods – for marlin perhaps?

Flying fish

# 17

## We first set foot in the United States of America – We are hit by a typhoon

On **Wednesday 8 July** it was exciting to have our first view of the North American coastline on our port side – the chart showed that we were off a narrow spit of land named Cape Hatteras which protruded from the line of the Atlantic eastern seaboard. Jack, in a nonchalant way, informed us that the area was nicknamed "The Graveyard of the Atlantic" because of its shoals and turbulent waters, its high risk for tropical storms and hurricanes. How reassuring!

Off this part of the Carolina coast the sea was strikingly green due to the shallowness of water over sand banks. We understood that part of this coast was a bird sanctuary. It seemed busy with many fishing boats.

On **Thursday 9 July** we put into Norfolk USA, on the south-eastern corner of Virginia, for essential purchases – fuel, fags and food. I went to the bank with Jack and cashed all my remaining $250 worth of travellers' cheques and gave the lot to Jack for the above necessities and to go toward repair of our radio. He gave me back $15 and most of that I gave to Duff for fags. Jack now owed me Barbados $364 as well as that day's US $250. Tobacco and cigars were purchased for Jack who said he had got cigarettes for Duff, although when we got back to the boat there were none for him.

It was 93°F in the shade on board. Chilled canned beer from the marina shop was particularly welcome and as Duff and I sat in the shade a lady came up to us and said how well and happy we looked and wanted to know all about our voyage. Norfolk was clearly a yachtsman's paradise and I was amazed by the multi-storage system for stacking craft, and all the excellent facilities.

Guy spent the best part of the day on the phone making arrangements in preparation for our arrival in New York. Jack became obstreperous with Huw and, indeed, with us all – for example, that Guy and I had apparently delayed the whole voyage by our bad steering!

It was brought to our notice by the electrician there in Norfolk that work that had been carried out by electricians in Whitby before we set off had been badly done. Apparently the two-way radio and our navigation system was not repairable because it had burnt-out due to having had two years of 24W power running through it when it should have had much less. (It seemed that YTS pupils had wired the entire boat back then.) Jack chose not to purchase a new system – I was sure because he could not afford to.

I phoned and got through to daughter Sally – bad news was that my bank O/D had reached its limit. Otherwise all was well.

"Duff is p----- off because of fag situation and the lack of an effective electrical navigation system for the rest of the voyage. He is considering leaving the boat when we reach New York".

We left Norfolk in bad order and in a hurry – Jack was so impatient to get away that he nearly left Guy behind – Guy had to leap for it and crashed himself hard against the stern in so doing. Jack was in a very aggressive mood – affected by bad news he had apparently received from England. He carelessly dragged the mooring pole adrift as he pulled away from the quayside. In the wheelhouse he perused the relevant chart of our whereabouts and issued our course instructions for continuing up the east coast.

However, we ran aground at 0115 on a shoal. We endured several extremely worrying hours during which we agonised over thoughts of ship-wreck, but thankfully floated free and put well out to sea. The chart spread on the table in the wheelhouse had shown no potential danger where we were located, but the charts were old and sand banks shift over time.

Jack related to us that Bella would rejoin the boat some time after New York – news that left me feeling uninspired.

At 2100 hours on **Saturday 11 July** I was awakened by Guy shaking me awake in my bunk. He said to follow him quickly, there was a storm brewing. Scrambling up the companionway after him and emerging on deck I was immediately struck by a weird stillness and silence which was completely at odds with the turbulent dynamics in the heavens above and around us. For this was one of nature's high dramas, an electrical storm, the entire night sky of deepest blackness pierced by jagged spikes of forked lightning with barely a pause between each splintering charge. What a spectacle! But then, breaking the silence, a few huge drops of rain pattered onto the wheelhouse roof – and within a trice, the *Helga Maria* was sucked into a maelstrom of ferocious violence and chaos, the storm was upon us with a crescendo of thunder, the sea pock-marked with sheets of incredibly heavy rain – the wave crests flattened by it, creating an un-naturally still sea considering the fury of the wind. The jib sail, which had been lying in the net, not lashed, was swept up, and immediately shredded before our disbelieving eyes. Within seconds I was drenched and clinging to the hand rail on the starboard side of the deck housing as the wind pinioned me helplessly against the bulkhead. I was shuddering with cold – but fascinated by the encompassing tumult. Hard to say how long it lasted – thirty minutes, forty? But then a warm wind returned and the tempest passed as suddenly as it had arrived.

Huw reported that while at the wheel he had seen on the radar screen the shadow of the storm rapidly approaching us, about three miles away to starboard. In spite of going hard to port, avoidance tactics were useless for once caught in the typhoon he was helpless at the helm for the tempest had the *Helga Maria* in its power as it whirled the boat around. It was an all-powerful, utterly un-nerving experience for us all. Huw was visibly shaken but calmly got us back on course again. Interviewed later by Guy, Huw confided how he had thought the boat must certainly be lost and how important it was not to show fright – something that so easily spreads to others – "you just do not show it."

As a panacea for all ills it seemed appropriate to have hot drinks all round. It was possible now to retrieve what was left of the damaged jib sail and investigate for any other damage, which, unbelievably, was minimal. Luckily the boat possessed spare sets of sails. Things went back to normal.

Duff became covered in spots all over his bottom, thighs and small of back. He had a headache and felt thoroughly unwell and completely drained. Nonplussed, I gave him an anti-allergy pill and enough for two per day till the symptoms hopefully desisted.

We reached Atlantic City harbour 1630 hours and spent approximately five hours there taking on oil, water and a few provisions. There was bickering and argument between Jack and Huw, an appearance of bad blood between them. The rest of us were OK and we were soon at sea again.

I lost part of a double tooth while nibbling nuts and had to put chewing gum in the hole to alleviate the sharpness rubbing my tongue sore.

Jack seemed to have been thinking a lot about my home

circumstances and thought I should alert the police when we returned to the UK, regarding the nuisance behaviours of my ex-lover. I considered the pros and cons of so doing and decided I would just have to wait and see how things developed.

# 18

# New York

On **Sunday 12 July** we reached New York, arriving after what was an exciting and spectacular run in for those of us to whom the iconic skyscraper frontage of the harbour had been only in the imagination. Unfortunately it was cloudy, with a swirling mist shrouding buildings one minute and revealing them the next, lending an air of mystery to the whole scene. We moored by an old wooden jetty in downtown South Street Seaport, which was a free berth for us thanks to Guy's earlier arrangements, this being a museum for vintage vessels. The mighty clipper ship *Peking* was beside us and was undergoing extensive conservation work. She completely dwarfed us with her mighty hull and towering masts. Our own vessel attracted much interest, and on the harbour side Duff, Huw and I met Maurice, a volunteer worker on the *Peking*. He later introduced us to his wife and daughter-in-law and the three of them proved to be extremely kind and hospitable. They took us on a four-hour whirlwind tour of the city, taking in China Town, a Jewish deli (where we ate pastrami sandwiches), the Empire State building, the city's gaol and so on, enabling us to absorb the flavour of this amazing, hectic maelstrom of humanity, with its whirling

Manhattan Island

traffic and hubbub, with wealth and poverty equally displayed, the harbour, the selling racket at the massive fish quay, the enormity of that metropolis, the variety. Mind-blowing for mariners like us, straight from the quiet of the ocean! Maurice took us home to his flat on the 18th floor of an apartment block. The views from the balcony, overlooking Manhattan and towards New Jersey were astounding from that height. His delightful wife prepared for us an afternoon tea of home-made chocolate brownies, ice cream and fruit salad. Maurice told us that, before retirement, his career had been as a furrier, as his father's had been in his homeland, the latter entering the United States as an immigrant through Staten Island.

We questioned Maurice about the *Peking* and he told us that she was the only one of her kind in America and that the conservation work on her was a very expensive project. He described her as a steel hulled four-masted barque belonging to the "Golden Age of Sail" of the mid 18th century, when the efficiency and use of commercial sailing vessels was at its peak. By the early 1920's steam boats had begun to take trade away from sail. These tall ships, and those who sailed them, were the last of their breed, sailing in the traditional way with few labour saving devices or safety features, often in extreme conditions. The clipper ships were the ultimate expression of grace and speed, often breaking speed records carrying cargoes of tea from China. The *Peking* was built in Hamburg in 1911 by Blohm and Voss and was operated by the company F.Laeisz. Her maiden voyage was between Europe and Valparaiso in Chile which probably took about eighty days doing approximately eighteen knots. She could carry a cargo of around 3,100 tons.

Maurice was passionate about his subject and to have been able to talk at greater length with him about the history of the *Peking* would have been a treat, but we unfortunately had to take our leave.

Jack gave me back $100 which enabled me to visit a dentist who put a temporary filling in my broken tooth. I bought, wrote and posted cards and purchased some provisions. We heard reports that eight hundred Russian sailors aboard four tall ships, all of them part of the Columbus flotilla, were stranded here by the financial problems of their homeland. Brooklyn's 800,000-strong Russian community had rallied round, showering the near starving sailors with gifts of food and clothes. But that would not enable them to return home – they did not have enough food or fuel for that voyage and their sails and ropes were rotten.

Maurice came aboard our boat in the evening and we had a party, Guy bringing a number of his New York friends. We sailed out to the Statue of Liberty to watch a stunning sunset settle over Manhattan. We talked and drank beers until the early hours, when our friends slowly began to drift away.

The next morning we briefly left port to sail out again to the Statue of Liberty and once we were appropriately positioned, Guy, from a borrowed rowing boat, took photographs and film of the *Helga Maria* with the Statue in the background.

We later left New York, our heads full of very happy memories of our sojourn there, and headed for Mystic Seaport, our next port of call. I cooked tea – corned beef, potatoes, onions all in the same pot, with caramelised carrots. We had been joined by a lady, whom Jack had befriended, called Debra. She had lost her husband two weeks previously and seemed adrift. She was to accompany us to Mystic, our next port up the coast, so I made up a bunk for her.

*Helga Maria* and the Statue of Liberty

# 19

## Mystic Seaport "Museum of America and the Sea"

On **Wednesday 15 July** we enjoyed a leisurely and scenically beautiful sail up the sound to Mystic Seaport, Connecticut. Mystic is named "The Museum of America and the Sea", a living history museum consisting of a village, ships and exhibits depicting coastal life in New England in the 19th century. It was founded in 1929. Duff and I met a lady called Dorothy who took us to the aquarium (where there were dolphins, which appalled me as I had become used to seeing them in their natural habitat) and to a smart bar where we had a couple of beers and complimentary cannelloni, crisps and dips. She later left us there and we continued to have a great time talking with the locals. It began to rain very hard and we eventually walked home, splashing through the puddles as we went like a couple of kids. We all eventually met up in the for'ard cabin and shared Huw's whisky. I became a little drunk and tearful and was slightly sick in my bunk into a saucepan.

Breakfast next morning was a stop and start affair as all the men were doing different things at different times. Inconveniently the privy had become full, almost to the point of overflowing, and had to be emptied into a large, lidded black bucket on deck, to be dealt with when we got out to sea again.

During the morning Guy filmed and interviewed us in the for'ard cabin for a film he proposed to make of our voyage up to that point. Huw, who had been sleeping, startled us when he flung open his bunk doors commanding that I must tell about the bad things as well as the good and joined in himself by stating a number of embarrassing truths, viz. Edna being a burden, Jack's financial problems, Jack's relationship with Bella, the complexities of the friendship between Duff and me, electrical failures and, generally, a compilation of factors leading to a narrowly avoided mutiny. All marvellous stuff for scandal mongers but not so good for a squeaky clean image! Jack refused to be interviewed initially but later granted Guy a brief one.

When the interviews were over to Guy's satisfaction he finally left us, for his work was in New York and it was time he went back to it. I knew I would miss his company, his steadiness and sanity, his fitness, capability and strength. The boat would be a poorer place without him, and we were now a useful crew member down.

Duff and I set out to explore the exhibits in Mystic village. The mode of dress for everyone working there was 19th century costume and the whole set-up took us into another world. We inspected the working preservation-shipyard with its blacksmiths, wood carvers and artisan craft people of all kinds. We went aboard the *Charles W. Morgan* – the last remaining wooden whaling ship in the world. I thought how sad it was that as a tourist attraction there was not one like it in Whitby harbour, with its long history of whaling and famous captains. We had a trip out on the steam boat *Sabina* and gloried in her immaculate engine room with its polished brass machinery and pistons. We were invited by Renee, the boat's buxom chief engineer, to return at 8.30pm to see the boat "put to bed", which we did and immediately after she whisked us in her car, very fast, to "John's Bar" for Guinness. Next morning we visited the supermarket to re-provision (what a joke when so short of money) and to get two gas cylinders from Mystic Ice and Fuel Company.

Jack eventually succeeded in starting the engine after an initial problem of leakage of compressed air from the cylinder.

Jack and Huw had had a "ding dong" the previous night apparently, and again that morning – I had seen Huw exasperatedly throw a tin of something at Jack's head, who, in anticipation, ducked at the right moment. It was all about Huw's perception of Jack's lack of organisation and equipment, his financial difficulties, his attitude toward people which could be very hard. Jack said he needed no-one and that was that. He had received, over the phone from Lynda in Whitby, the disappointing news that at the present time there was no contract forthcoming for the making of the film of his 1991 voyage to the Arctic. Jack had been pinning his hopes on its going ahead because that could have solved a lot of his financial headaches.

Duff had the offer of a job in Mystic, for October, if he wanted it, and was required to fill in a relevant form. Well, New England might have made a new start for him, but in the event he declined the idea.

At 1500 hours we left Mystic and were heading for Halifax, Nova Scotia. The notorious Nantucket shoals were on our port side, that area of dangerously shallow water that extends from Nantucket Island, Massachusetts, into the Atlantic for 23 miles eastward and south-eastward for 40 miles. The shoals are constantly changing due to strong tidal currents of a rotary character. In places the water depth is no more than three feet. Numerous ships have been wrecked, notably, in 1976, the oil tanker *Argo Merchant*. It was reassuring to leave that no-go area well to port.

Visibility was poor with a lumpy sea. I was wearing shirt, jumper, jeans, long wool socks and boots. We were necessarily now on a six hour watch regime – six hours on, six hours off, and so on, since there were now only four of us to crew. It was a bit disorienting after what we'd been used to.

Huw made breakfast, I washed up. I made lunch and washed up. Afterward I painted the bulkheads either side of the door in galley alley. Visibility was only about twenty five yards in swirling mist. Duff made tea – ham, potatoes, sauerkraut, olives, beetroot, pumpernickel and banana sauce.

Duff had no cigarettes, saying he could commit suicide one minute and then becoming absorbed in his cooking and seeming to forget about his craving the next. I only had five dollars left for the entire voyage until Jack reimbursed me, so could do no more than purchase two packs of cigarettes for him which were soon smoked. That meant another seven or eight days of misery for him (and for us).

**Sunday 19 July** at 0850 hours showed us thick fog for Duff's and my early watch, necessitating sounding the horn at regular intervals. Everything was dripping wet caused by the heavy drenching dew. This was a testing time indeed – Duff in a diabolical frame of mind, Huw very deaf and cantankerous, Jack *comme ci, comme ca*, me, well, certainly I found the new regime more demanding. Work in the galley was ghastly. I was nonplussed as to how I was to make a good nourishing soup. I battled to get rid of grease, battled to know what to do with some of the left-over food. It was chilly, my clothes felt damp. Grey weather, grey mood, bone ache in joints, feet hurt in my boots.

I applied more white paint in galley alley, and yellow paint to freshen up our storage accommodation area. Additionally, all metal work on the boat rusted very quickly and needed constant rubbing down and touching up.

Duff was not acknowledging or speaking to me at all – nicotine deprivation seemed to be causing him to eat vast quantities of bread and to look intent upon murder.

But, we had a wonderful end to a bleak day – we were surrounded by schools of bottle nose dolphins dipping and diving across our bows and squeaking all around us – I watched them from the net to get up close. One swam on its side at intervals and seemed to be viewing me with one eye. I finished work in the galley and lashed the sails at 2000 hours. It had been a tiring day.

On **Monday 20 July** I arose at 0720 hours to learn of trouble with the electrical system again so that we now had no radar, no lights, and no form of electrical navigation. In fog, in strange and hazardous shoal waters, and with shipping around, this was seriously not good news and was yet another potential delay and danger for us and a creator of tension. I wore a whistle round my neck so that when on watch in the bow I could alert Duff at the helm of any hazard.

While chatting on deck with Jack he told me of three ships, on which he had served in the past, which had been lost – one had been rammed, one caught fire through electrical fault and another was lost on rocks off Trinidad. Well, I thought, that's three catastrophes over and done with, hopefully there won't be any more! He also vouchsafed to me that it could be a very lonely place being the skipper, and that he missed Bella with whom he had been able to share some of his anxieties.

I worked below decks in accommodation, tidying and re-organising our food supplies. Dolphins were around our bows again which was cheering, although the thick fog persisted with its attendant anxieties.

On **Tuesday 21 July** I came off watch at 0800 hours deciding to ignore the chill by having a strip and hair wash, and was rewarded by feeling much better for it. It was often tempting, when tired, to fall into one's bunk fully clothed and unwashed.

It had dripped with mist all night, but hazy sun began to show through by morning. I had quite enjoyed the watch but it had been worrying because of collision potential with having no port, starboard or masthead lights. Duff made breakfast – porridge, followed by pancakes, beans and eggs. Delicious and most welcome.

A large white gull with brown, white edged wings circled the boat and accompanied us for quite a distance. Its continuing presence with us for several days reminded me of the moving poem by Samuel Taylor Coleridge, *The Rime of the Ancient Mariner*, which tells of a following albatross shot dead with a cross bow resulting in great misfortune for the ship and her crew. However, our bird was no albatross and we carried no weapon.

During the night of **22 July** at 0400 hours, Huw became very much the worse for drink in the for'ard cabin which he shared with Duff, and was shouting "who's pee-ed in my bucket?" and "I am very disappointed that all my whisky has gone", completely disturbing Duff's sleep. Duff finally escaped to the empty bunk below mine and slumbered soundly.

# 20

## Halifax, Nova Scotia

On **Wednesday 22 July** I awoke to find that we were already heading up the estuary leading to the port of Halifax, Nova Scotia. We were blessed with a beautiful, sunny, clear morning.

We were warmly welcomed into the harbour and given a free berth in what was a museum of vintage vessels. There was massive interest in the *Helga Maria*. The quayside swarmed with wonderfully friendly people talking, talking, talking and so interested in us and our voyage and offering help, support and hospitality during our stay.

Jack gave an interview for Tyne Tees TV which had sent a representative to meet us.

Duff cooked scrambled eggs for our breakfast. I spent a busy morning stripping all bunks, airing all mattresses and gathering dirty laundry to take to a launderette. I washed the bunks down with "Smell o' Pine" and tidied up generally in preparation for the possible arrival of the Rev. Paul Burkitt, Lynda and Bella who might join us on Sunday. We partook of soup and French fries for lunch.

While Jack busied himself with jobs on board, Duff and I went to the Citadel Military Museum. The present Citadel was built in

1856 and named Fort George after King George 2nd and is situated on the top of a large hill overlooking the harbour. Originally, in the 18th century, the British Military had recognised that the harbour could easily be defended and so in 1749 founded a town there, the early settlers building their homes at the base of the hill close to the water, with a wooden guardhouse built on the top of the hill. At the museum we also learned of the devastating explosion which had wrecked the Richmond area of the city in 1917.

Duff said he could not find the fags Huw had bought for him so he was wretched again, settling down to sleep on the day bed in the mess. I stayed with him for a while but then retired for the night to my bunk. I cared for the man so much and it hurt me that I could not see a way of helping him. I didn't know what to do.

**Friday 24 July** – I was up at 0800 hours. Courtesy of new friend, museum boss Graham, I phoned my daughter Sally from the Maritime Museum office and asked her to make arrangements for further kennelling of my dog, Clem, since it was clear that it would be at least another month before we were home. She had most obligingly put money into my bank account, so I withdrew $200 from the bank there as I was out of funds. Graham took us to the launderette in his car and while the wash ensued took us on a tour of the town and its environs. The mainly wooden houses were painted in fresh, bright colours, everywhere neat as a new pin and we gained the impression of a happy, friendly community.

Duff and I went out in the evening with Ben Tremblay, a young Appalachian harp player whom we had met on the quay side. The instrument I had not heard before and found the sound of it delightful. He came back to the boat with us and we had a party in Huw's cabin to the accompaniment of his music, which I recorded.

Graham gave Duff a photocopy of Frederick J. Pohl's book entitled *Prince Henry Sinclair – His Expedition to the New World in 1398*, and other bits and pieces relevant to that voyage made ninety four years previous to that of Columbus. Duff was overjoyed because he already had some knowledge of that earlier voyage having spent time at Rosslyn Chapel, just South of Edinburgh, talking to the custodian there. Rosslyn Castle, adjacent to the Chapel, is the ancient seat of the Sinclairs, an eminent Scottish family, and where Prince Henry grew up. He was created Earl of Orkney and Lord of Shetland by King Haakon of Norway in 1379. His voyage was with a fleet of 13 vessels, at least 200 men and an Italian navigator, Antonio Zeno. He sailed, taking a northerly route, quite different from that of Columbus, from the Orkney Islands to Newfoundland and from thence into the heartland of Nova Scotia. He lived in harmony with the indigenous Mi'kmaq Indians, over-wintering with them, and teaching them how to fish with nets. He so impressed them that he became the inspiration for their legends of the Man/God Glooscap. In 1399 he sailed on into what is now Massachusetts before returning to the Orkneys where he died in battle defending his country.

Duff and I, when on watch together in the wheelhouse, had talked about the story a great deal since leaving Whitby, a story which was so very different from that of Christopher Columbus, the latter representing greed for gold, for slavery and for appalling genocide – his arrival in the Bahamas having decimated the indigenous Indian population to near extinction.

I made up all the bunks with clean linen in preparation for the expected influx. Jack had arranged for our gaff, storm damaged by earlier bad weather, to receive some essential repairs, and, the work now completed, was readying it for use by lacing the sail back on and organising the halyards and topping lift.

Eric, Second Mate from the training ship *Concordia* moored close to us, invited us, on the morrow, to watch a video of the clipper ship *Peking* rounding the Horn. This would certainly be of particular interest to us, having been moored beside her in New York and learned something of her story.

I wrote some cards and stayed on the boat all day talking to people and listening to Jack – he was spinning many a good yarn, entertaining those on the quayside and anyone who came aboard. Duff was reading about Prince Henry and sleeping a great deal.

Huw and I treated Jack and Duff to an evening meal at "Lower Deck" in town and afterwards Duff and I went to "O'Carrols" pub to listen to folk music, drink beer and talk with the locals. The Scottish influence was very noticeable and there was clearly great pride in the Scottish ancestry. Duff, as a Scot, was particularly interested in the stories of early settlement there:

"The first settlement was in 1621 when King James 6th of Scotland granted permission to William Alexander, 1st Earl of Stirling, to establish a settlement in Canada. This settlement was called Nova Scotia – New Scotland.

Dense forest had to be cleared before shelters could be built, but there was a lack of practical skills and their first winter was wretched, plagued by bitter cold, disease and scurvy. Out of the original seventy, thirty had died before their first spring. War with France made the colony impossible to maintain for French blockades stopped supplies getting in, coupled with attacks from nearby French colonies. Many returned home or moved to New England.

In 1773 a Scots passenger ship, the *Hector*, arrived in Pictou, carrying one hundred and seventy Highlanders and ten men from Greenock. Most were Gaelic speakers. The settlers had been encouraged to emigrate by offer of free passage, supplies for a year and free land grants. They spent eleven long weeks at sea, suffering outbreaks of dysentery and smallpox which claimed the lives of eighteen children. They set about building shelters against the upcoming winter, but the supplies never came. Their first winter was desperate, but they stayed. Once a Gaelic speaking colony was established entire Highland villages started to arrive.

In 1812, Hector, 22nd Chief of the clan McLean, moved to Nova Scotia with five hundred of his clansmen

and neighbours. Around 15,000 Scots emigrated to
Canada between 1770 and 1815, mainly from the
Highlands and Islands and largely because back home in
the north of Scotland the clans people, in their ancestral
glens, were being ruthlessly driven from their homes to
make way for Cheviot sheep – the notorious Highland
Clearances."

(The above copied into my journal. Source forgotten.)

We understood how proudly the Scottish roots had been
maintained there in Nova Scotia and how the Gaelic language
and music flourished there – it felt almost more Scotland than
Scotland.

We had been having a happy time there – no excess booze
or arguments – what a difference it made. There was a feeling of
calm content although Huw was clearly homesick and missing
Lil, Jack had his financial problems looming for when he got
home, and I had issues which would need sorting out too, but
they were certainly not at the fore front of my brain just then,
quite the reverse. Duff was much more settled, calm, reading
about the Sinclair voyage. There was strong support there in
Halifax to promote plans for celebrations of the 600th anniversary
of Sinclair's voyage and for the erection of a monument at Eliza
Point, Guysborough, where Sinclair dropped anchor on June
1st, 1398. Duff had greatly enjoyed meeting and chatting with
octogenarian Tim who was deeply involved in the Sinclair project.

In the afternoon Duff and I went aboard the *Concordia* as
arranged the previous day, where we watched the stunning video of
*Around the Horn*. The video was from the original 16 mm footage
filmed on board the *Peking* by Irving Johnson in 1929 – film that
at the time shocked both experienced Cape Horn veterans and
landsmen alike at the extreme conditions the *Peking* experienced.
Cape Horn, at the southern tip of South America, is at the

confluence of the three oceans, the Atlantic, the Pacific and the Antarctic, and one of the most treacherous stretches of sea on the globe. Apart from her captain, the ship would have been manned by a first and a second mate and between twenty or thirty seamen. They worked a punishing regime of four hours on, four hours off, twenty four hours a day for the entire length of the voyage, which could have been up to a hundred days.

I was completely captivated and impressed by the film. We also learned a little more regarding the story of the *Peking*. During the 1914–18 War she was in Valparaiso in Chile and after it she was awarded to Italy as war reparation. In 1923 she was sold back to her original owners, the Laeisz brothers, and continued to trade. In 1932 she was sold into Great Britain and re-named the *Arethusa*. During World War 2 she was in the Royal Navy as *H.M.S. Pekin* but retired in 1975 and sold to Jack Aron for the South Street Seaport Museum – which is where we first had the privilege of encountering her.

Duff cooked a meal for us all, Jack, Huw, and the newly arrived Bella, but they decided to eat out. Duff and I went to "O'Carrol's" bar for some drinks and to listen to music, later joining Huw for a wee dram in his cabin. He had been very upset by something Bella had flippantly said, about what Lil might be up to while he was away. Disgusted, he had come back on his own.

On **Tuesday 28 July** Jack let us know that Lynda and Paul Burkitt would not be joining us in Halifax. News from home was that there was a lot of press about us, largely resulting from the film which Guy had made and which had been shown on Tyne Tees TV and been very well received. There was still no money in the offing for Duff – it continued to be a rotten situation for him – being dependent on Huw and me for drinks and fags whenever we were in port. Those items were expensive there – beer $3.50 a pint and fags $7 a packet. There was trouble with the alternator – yet another electrical problem to have reared its ugly head.

Jack took on a new crew member, Sam, appearing to be a reasonably intelligent young man. He had been unemployed for a while but had previously worked for fisheries, checking the catches on fishing boats, and purportedly enjoyed being at sea. He wanted to accompany us back to the UK, intending to explore Scotland for as long as his money lasted. Short-handed as we had been since losing Guy at Mistic Seaport I felt relieved that we now had someone who would be able, hopefully, to replace him.

I cooked a chicken meal, and afterwards Duff, Sam and I talked about Henry Sinclair.

Next morning I made porridge and washed up last night's pots. Huw cooked eggs, bacon and beans, a satisfying breakfast, but I felt low in spirit – I felt I had to be prepared for Duff's easing himself out of my life and I knew I would find it hard to adjust to that. He was talking of spending the winter in Halifax to do research on Henry Sinclair. He also talked of living with the Mi'kmaqu for a while. He had had a premonition years ago that he would live with Indians and it looked as though that *could* come to fruition. He had received an offer for accommodation aboard the *Arcadia* for the winter if he could find employment or sponsorship. His life was evolving in a most interesting manner and I was so glad for him – but none of it involved me. So, what the hell, I had felt all along that I was just a stepping stone for him to something else.

Bella and I went to the bank and then to Scotia Square to shop for the boat and buy whisky for Huw. We each had a shower in the Museum under-croft during the afternoon and felt the better for it.

Duff worked all morning on the alternator/electrics with a new acquaintance, David Reed, a qualified electrician who had kindly volunteered to check the system thoroughly for us. David was a classical guitarist, and, additionally, was an adventuresome man who told us he had sailed round the world, taking eight years to do so. We did meet some amazing people. I was worried about time running out for me to resume work at the hospital – I didn't want to find that I had been sacked! I had originally received four months' sabbatical from the hospital and I had already exceeded that time. I did not know how long we might have to stay in Halifax while the electrics were fixed and I had overheard Jack mentioning careening and caulking to the hull. Would I have to fly home from here?

Later in the morning Ben Tremblay came aboard with his harp and David Reed got out his guitar and there was a wonderful impromptu gathering on deck of men talking about and playing their instruments and singing. Bella joined in with her flute. Huw, not to be outdone, gave a rendering of *The Green Eye of the Little Yellow God*.

The next day I went with Duff and Sam to the Art Gallery to see the exhibition of folk art, and afterwards strolled in the Victorian Park. I bought felt liners for Duff's sea boots and Nova Scotia badges for our caps. Sam presented us with a book about the munitions disaster in 1917 which destroyed much of Halifax.

By afternoon the electrics appeared to have been sorted out to David Reed's satisfaction, thank goodness, and so, caulking and careening postponed, we left Halifax harbour at 0300 hours to a wonderful send off – Tim, Graham, David Reed, Ben, *et al.* What good people they all were.

The quiet sea unexpectedly showed phosphorescence – I was surprised to see it in this colder clime.

I cooked tea while the men and Bella put up the sails. We ate beef stew, onions in white sauce with sage, fresh carrots and cabbage.

Afterwards, I decided to read about the Munitions Disaster from Sam's book.

Now, all these years later, and through the web-site 'History', I am vivdly reminded of what I learned back then of how:

"At 9.05 hours on December 6 1917 in the harbour of Halifax, Nova Scotia, the most devastating man-made explosion in the pre-atomic age occurred when SS 'Mont Blanc', a French munitions ship, exploded 20 minutes after colliding with another vessel.

As WW1 raged in Europe, the port city of Halifax bustled with ships packed with troops, relief supplies and munitions to cross the Atlantic. The morning of Dec. 6 the Norwegian vessel 'Imo' left its mooring in the harbour for New York. At the same time the freighter 'Mont Blanc', its cargo hold packed with highly explosive munitions – 2,300 tons of picric acid, 200 tons of TNT, 35 tons of high octane gasoline and ten tons of gun cotton – was forging through the harbour's narrows to join a military convoy that would escort it across the Atlantic.

At approximately 0845 hours the two ships collided, setting the picric acid ablaze. The 'Mont Blanc' was propelled towards the shore by its collision and the crew rapidly abandoned ship, attempting, without success, to alert the harbour of the peril of the burning ship. Spectators gathered along the waterfront to watch the spectacle and minutes later it brushed by a harbour pier, setting it ablaze. The fire department responded quickly and was positioning its engine next to the nearest hydrant when the 'Mont Blanc' exploded at 0905 in a blinding white flash.

The massive explosion killed more than 1,800 people, injuring another 9,000, blinding 200 and destroyed almost the entire north end of the city of Halifax including more than 1,600 homes. The resulting shock wave shattered windows 50 miles away and the sound of the explosion could be heard hundreds of miles away. "

Citation: The Great Halifax Explosion. URL https:/www.history.com/this-day-in-history/the-great-halifax-explosion

Sam's book continued to describe in detail the devastating effects of the explosion, the resulting hardships for the homeless and the gradual recovery from the event. The tragedy is forever hard-wired into the consciousness of Halifax.

# 21

## Heading along the Breton coast toward Newfoundland

During **Thursday 31 – Saturday 1 August** we progressed along the Breton Island coast, now heading for Newfoundland. There was no wind, the sea was a flat calm and we had to resort to the engine. Duff took down the two mainsails. All watches were un-remarkable apart from the sighting of a pod of pilot whales, but they were not with us for long. For tea Duff glazed a tinned ham and served it with mashed green beans, corn and peas – delicious.

On **Sunday 2 August** middle watch *was* remarkable for we were struck by a force 8 gale, lashing rain, with big seas breaking over the boat. I donned my thermal vest and long johns under my upper gear, wound a towel round my neck, put on thick socks plus wellington boots and oil skins. Duff wore a polythene bag on his head which was aesthetically displeasing, but effective. We had now to keep a lookout for the presence of ice floes in this more northerly clime, but saw none. Visibility was very poor. It was hard work doing any jobs, as we needed both hands for hanging on. The *Helga Maria* was taking the seas well. I was eventually glad to retire to my, albeit wet, bunk, thinking how thankful I was for the thermal sleeping bag that daughter Sally had lent me, which was, mercifully, waterproof. I arose next morning to find that conditions had settled and become dry. On our port side the coast of Newfoundland was now in view. Our course was 090° east, and it felt cold. Wet clothes, oilskins and boots were hung and scattered all over the mess, proper drying facilities were zero. Drips were appearing in numerous new places particularly around the deck lights, one of which, of course, was immediately above my bunk! Huw abandoned his now wet and unusable bunk in the for'ard cabin, deciding to try out what had been Adie's bunk in the starboard cabin mid-ships.

Bella seemed tired and said she was not sleeping.

Young Sam was coping fine – a nice chap and fitting in well with all of us. I had discovered that he was an animal lover, so he and I started on a good footing.

For tea we had Huw's "stew" which had been hurling itself over the galley floor all day, due to the crazy motion of the boat. It was the remains of Duff's yesterday's curry, which had been scheduled for lunch and had tins of tomatoes and kidney beans added – but Huw incorporated still more and more in desperation as it continued to spill itself over the deck.

We also made a dish of fresh shredded cabbage with garlic, red kidney beans and shredded apple all tossed together.

Huw's soups (alias stews) had been a lunch time mainstay but had been extravagant, getting thicker and thicker as the weeks went by. They were not what I liked to eat before afternoon watch, Bella did not eat it because she was a vegetarian, Sam ate practically nothing, so the huge, ever expanding pot-full was never completely consumed. The previous day Jack had emptied the pot over the side because he was sick of it, but before we knew where we were there was another huge pan of it. The remains of breakfast porridge went in, so did any left-over rice, potatoes and vegetables from the previous meal, but Huw went on emptying tins and cartons of dried meat into it so that it ended up as a very extravagant meal.

I showed a spark of unreasonable jealousy/cattiness towards Duff one evening. I deeply regretted it, for he seemed visibly to shrink but I was hurt by his continued coolness toward me when we were off watch whilst being relaxed and chatty with everyone else. I should have been used to it by now.

My journal entry of **Monday 3 August** states that my nose was dripping with the cold although there was sun and blue sky with mere wisps of cloud. The deck was littered with drying clothes. The coast of Newfoundland on our port side showed us rocky cliffs and barren grey-green unpopulated land. Due to there being no wind we were under engine power.

Anarchy at lunch time! – Huw's soup/stew remained largely uneaten. Bella ate cheese and marmalade. I had two boiled eggs with rye bread, Duff ate nothing, I didn't know about Sam, so only Jack and Huw ate soup.

It felt too cold for a strip-wash now so morning ablutions were kept to a minimum. I wondered if Sam would be driven eventually to growing a beard, for I timed him one day spending one and a quarter hours over a shave in a bucket of sea water with no visible lather. How long would he be able to maintain such meticulous attention to his chin? Jack was stomping up and down the deck, up and down. What was on his mind, I wondered?

Bella prepared fishing lines, but Jack would not linger for her to try them out as, apparently, Lynda would be waiting for us in St. John's, our next port in Newfoundland. She would re-join us there for the final crossing of the Atlantic as we set off for home. At 1650 hours the rocky Newfoundland coastline showed us pine forests and small settlements.

Duff made a tea of haggis and pancakes.

Bella was scraping the fore-mainmast prior to varnishing and I was applying linseed oil to the scratched locker top which served us as a table aft.

# 22

## St. John's, Newfoundland

On **Tuesday 4 August** at midnight we entered St. John's large natural harbour through its dramatic entrance between high rocky cliffs on either side. We were guided by three green leading lights but were unable to find our berth at first and it was 0200 hours before we finally tied up.

I was awakened next morning by strong winds driving fine gravel and dust onto the decks – from my bunk it sounded like heavy rain or hail showering down upon us.

We moved to our proper berth, later meeting up with Lynda, and it was really great to see her again.

She'd arrived there a couple of nights before and stayed in a hotel to await our arrival. Huw and I could not help feeling apprehensive about how Lynda would react to the altered dynamics of our now sea-worn crew from which she had parted company so long ago in Falmouth.

Some of us went to a bar or two at lunchtime and found excellent draught Guinness and Smithwick's ale. Sam and I went for showers at the university on the kind invitation of a lecturer Sam had met there.

I went out in the evening with Sam and Duff and a chap they'd met. There was a lot of loud music and Guinness but we were not really in the mood, having been out at lunchtime and most of the afternoon. We went back to the boat and had nightcaps with Huw in the for'ard cabin – the best part of the night. Lynda joined us for a while. Huw had had a chat with her about events in the Caribbean, the threatened mutiny and general discontent. She was upset – shocked by how divided we had become, how subdued. I went to bed at 0230. I was up at 0900 hours and made porridge which only I ate! Lynda, feeling upset and with much to think about, went for a walk. Later she and Jack went out together and talked at length. Bella was hanging about like a spare part so she, Huw, Duff and I went to a bar for Guinness where we spent most of the afternoon. I would have liked to go to the museum. I was spending all my money on booze and fags for Duff – what sort of a fool was I? I was a fool in love.

In the early evening, like a lucky charm, Kevin Gould turned up. Kevin was the husband of one of my Casualty colleagues, Sally Gould. He had heard that we were in St. John's and had searched for where we were moored. He was working there on the construction of oil rigs. He took Sam and me to his apartment where we did lots of clothes washing and while I had a bath he cooked spaghetti bolognese, followed by strawberries and cream, coffee, biscuits and brandy. We had a LOVELY evening and got back to the boat at 1230.

On **Thursday 6 August** Kevin took us in his car to the Cabot Tower, situated at the top of Signal Hill, which commanded incredible views over St. John's and the sea. The morning was overcast with grey clouds scudding before a fresh wind over a grey and choppy sea. The construction of the tower began in 1898 to commemorate the 400th anniversary of John Cabot's discovery of Newfoundland and also of Queen Victoria's Diamond Jubilee. It was opened in 1900. It stood fifteen metres high, was of Gothic Revival style and was designed by St. John's architect, William Howe Green.

In 1901 Signal Hill was at the centre of a major international breakthrough. On 12 December of that year, in a blustering gale at Signal Hill, the scientist, Guglielmo Marconi, and his assistants, launched an aerial suspended at 500 feet from a kite. From the atmospherics the aerial received the very first transatlantic wireless signal – the letter "S" in Morse code, transmitted from Poldhu in Cornwall, Great Britain. Marconi's achievement led to a new age in communication technology.

From a booklet I picked up at the Tower, compiled by Pam Reynolds, 1984, for the Marconi Company Limited, I learned the following:

"Marconi was born in 1874 in Bologna, Italy. He showed little interest in schooling, preferring to work in the attic at home devising scientific toys. His dream was to use Hertzian waves as a basis for communicating without wires. By early 1895 he had succeeded in transmitting signals over a few yards of space using a Morse key. By August 1895 he achieved transmission over a distance of one and three quarter miles. The Italian government showed no interest so he set sail for England and in 1896 he there filed the world's first patent application for a system of telegraphy using Hertzian waves. He achieved communication across the Bristol Channel – 8.7 miles. Then the Solent was spanned. The Italian Navy now adopted Marconi wireless. Queen Victoria at Osborne House could communicate with the Prince of Wales aboard the Royal Yacht in the Solent. In 1899 wireless was installed on three Royal Navy ships and was brought into service during the South African War. Marconi then planned to span the Atlantic. 1900 saw the birth of The

Marconi International Marine Communication Company Ltd.

In 1914, at the outbreak of hostilities with Germany the importance of wireless as an instrument of war was immediately recognised, and the Admiralty at once assumed control of the Marconi works. Marconi's wireless telegraphists performed an invaluable service in all the armed forces and the merchant navy, both as operators and as training officers."

My father had served throughout WW1 in the merchant navy as a Marconi wireless officer. He continued in this employment until 1926, sailing in a variety of vessels all around the world. Consequently I was much impressed and interested to learn the above information while at the Cabot Tower.

Kevin lent me his car phone which enabled me to make contact with family, which was wonderful, and afterwards took Bella and me back to his flat where she had a bath and I relaxed in the comforting warmth of his living room (to which we were unused and found almost too much!). When he returned us to the fresh air and our friend, the boat, he bade us farewell for we were to leave St. John's on the morrow. What wonderful friendship he had shown us.

My journal tells that:

"I am pervaded by a strange mood. A sense of loss I think, now that we are approaching the final part of our voyage and that all of this will just be a mere memory once we are home. My mind is also tinged with some apprehension – wondering what weather conditions we may meet in the north Atlantic. One hears all sorts of tales – none good".

Later in the day Duff and I revisited various Welsh and Irish pubs, allowing the unique St. John's ambience and its music wash around us, committing it all to our memory banks.

Next morning I was able to fit in a visit to the museum which was mainly devoted to the culture of the Mi'kmaq and indigenous Algonkian speaking peoples. I learned that before the arrival of the first Europeans they led a semi-nomadic existence, living in extended family groups and exploiting seasonal food supplies. They had mastered techniques which enabled them to manufacture the necessities of life from animal bone, ivory, teeth and claws, shells, quills, hair and feathers, fur and leather; from clays and native copper, from stone, wood, roots, bark and plants – nothing was wasted. From the moose, for example, they had taken the blood, meat and marrow for food, and the fur and hides for clothing. Moose brains were used in tanning skins, antlers were worked into tools, dew claws became rattles, the shin bone was carved into dice, the hair used in embroidery, and the tendons became sewing thread. Even the hoofs were important – as an ingredient in a remedy for epilepsy. Birch bark was utilised to cover their wigwams and to construct their canoes. Unfortunately the advent of Europeans adversely affected the Mi'kmaq culture and population, bringing about the abandonment of many techniques and materials that had been in existence for centuries.

Research was ongoing to recover as much as possible of early Mi'kmaq culture and forgotten richness of their art – of the ingenuity, the craftsmanship and the eye for beauty that is part of the heritage of those peoples.

I found time to send a final postcard to my friends in Casualty, which read:

"Well, this is the last post before the final transatlantic crossing. Hope we don't bump into any icebergs. There was cold and stormy weather between Halifax and here. It won't be long now before this wrinkled old prune will be back".

Quite incredibly, while I was at the museum, Duff had a telephone conversation with the current chief of the Mi'kmaq! He declined to tell me of the dialogue between them but he seemed a happy man.

# 23

## The second transatlantic crossing

*"It is not the beginning but of the continuing of the same until it be thoroughly finished that yieldeth the true glory"*
From an old calendar

We left St. John's at 1730 hours on **8 August**. We gathered around Jack on deck as he read a beautiful prayer for our safe voyage home. I found it very moving. I was tense against this moment of finally setting off for home – I was a jumble of mixed feelings, the end of an idyll on the one hand, but, on the other, I was able to think of it as a new beginning. I quickly began to feel better, stronger and more positive. We all partook of a tot of rum, and we were away, into a brilliantly sunny and warm afternoon. Marvellous feeling, as always, just to be at sea again, leaving the city and dust and human mess behind and be heading for the pure, open sea. When in port, and the shipboard routine gone to pot, the variety of public houses inevitably drew us like a magnet, which was fun at the time, but I for one always felt healthier when at sea! Nevertheless, I had a couple of cans of ale tucked behind my pillow which would, no doubt, be enjoyed at some stage.

We ate a late tea aft, at the locker top, and we lingered there in the stern to witness a departing gift from Newfoundland – a wonderful sunset, the most magnificent we had witnessed so far. The sun dropped dramatically behind the dark, high, craggy cliffs and the vivid glow lingered all the way along the shore-land and spilled out and over the sea. I was awakened next morning, long before my getting-up time, by a shout, "Get up Rosie, there's an iceberg, you mustn't miss it". I stumbled from my bunk onto the deck and there it was, rather in the distance but still appearing impressively massive, crystalline and dazzlingly white in the brilliant sunshine with fissures in its side reflecting hues of turquoise- blue. It appeared strangely lonesome floating there completely on its own.

Two dead whales had been sighted earlier – a sad and total mystery, cause of death unknown.

The sky that morning was azure, streaked with just the merest wisps of high cloud – the sun warm but the air very cool. The sea was quiet, engine on, no sails. There were flocks of fulmars feeding on bread we threw for them.

I washed my hair, which blew dry in the wind, and I felt refreshed. Yesterday had been a long day and the routine seemed to have gone to pot – galley disorganised, no washing up done, no lunch made. Huw, clearly, was glad to be back at sea, the sea that he admitted had always drawn him like a magnet; but now he was winging his way back to his beloved Lil and I think he'd waived aside such mundane things as lunch or washing up – he'd been homesick for so long and just longing to be back with that lady of his and share breakfast with her on their patio.

At midnight on middle watch on **9 August** there was a clear, starry, moonlit sky, bitterly cold with heavy dew. Duff and I made careful half hourly lookouts, turn and turn about so as not to get too cold, and saw no icebergs. The sea was very quiet. At 0400 hours it was a relief to get into my thermal sleeping bag to get warm.

I slept till 0930 hours, consuming two bowls of porridge with brown sugar while Jack imparted the news to me that Huw had had to go off watch. He was sweating, got the shakes, couldn't eat and gone to his bunk. Was this a chill or due to alcohol, I wondered? What to do about it? Should I confiscate his booze? It was surely my responsibility to do what Lil would do in the circumstances which, I guessed, would be confiscation. Hopefully I wouldn't have to make the difficult decision.

It became a very hot, sunny morning and I was in shorts and bare feet. Jack was busy in the crow's nest, scraping and painting while Bella was at the wheel. She was very quiet these days – a difficult time for her as she had become used to having Jack all to herself and now his erstwhile adviser and "rock", in the shape of Lynda, was back amongst us. Lynda's chats with Jack, Huw and me had helped her gain a perspective on events and she seemed in balance now and adjusted to the way things were. Jack was cheerful and later joined Bella at the fishing but nothing was caught or seen.

Duff was quiet just then and seemed abstracted, his mind full of the Sinclair project. Sam was great and I found him to be good company when our paths crossed.

Me? I was feeling strong and of clear mind, able to look forward to returning home and reuniting with my dog, Clem. All would be well.

Following our course of 090° east we had covered 180 nautical miles since leaving St. John's, which augured well for us – BUT – we still had a long way to go and unknown conditions to face. Ten icebergs had been sighted during the various watches since we'd left St. John's and I was shocked to hear that *six* dead whales had been seen by Russian fishing boats, cause of death, again, unknown.

On **Monday 10 August** Duff made an excellent tea out of the chickens Lynda and I had purchased in St. John's, flavouring them with orange and lemon, serving them with rice, and followed by a chocolate pudding.

Our middle watch was uneventful, bitterly cold with heavy

dew. Duff was not feeling well now but the bottle of whisky Jack gave us "on the house" helped his symptoms greatly and he and I chatted happily together in the mess until we went to our bunks at 0600 hours. I checked on Huw, still sweating heavily and looking puffy in his face – to settle his fever I gave him paracetamol to take five hourly, and a clean, dry duvet and pillows.

I found the opportunity myself to have a good long talk with Lynda about the voyage generally, and Jack. She was obviously disappointed by how Jack had become so close to Bella since he had been dead against couples from the outset, but had decided to shrug her shoulders about the affair and just get on with things.

Information regarding our departure from St. John's and our future plans for arrival back in the UK had been leaked to the press, possibly by the harbourmaster. Jack subsequently received a message from the police for him to phone his agent back home. Jack did so and was advised not to go home via the Caledonian Canal to Whitby (as was his intention) if he wished to avoid being met by the D.O.T. who were now alerted to our movements and plans. Jack certainly did not wish to meet them, having fallen foul of them in the past, and they, I assumed, had further bones to pick with him. So, no doubt, he would come up with alternative plans for entry into the UK. He appeared to be shouldering the news well enough and was up the mainmast, still scraping and painting around the crow's nest.

General maintenance tasks continued – Sam was painting the roof of the deck-housing green, Bella was re-whipping the stays on the bowsprit which supported the net, and Lynda was sanding the gunwale tops and re-varnishing them. Huw was still unwell and had not left his bunk.

I developed a sore gland in my throat and I remembered that before we left St. John's, Huw, Duff and I foolishly, as it turned out, spent an evening in a Welsh bar with an Australian who had an appallingly heavy cold. That would explain the origin of our maladies! The arrangements were that if a crew member was ill and had to go off watch, it was up to the others to cover that watch, so that morning Jack worked a six hour watch followed by Duff and I doing likewise, instead of our customary four hour watches.

While at the helm, and as it required little attention just then due to a quiet sea, I idly sketched onto a blank page in my journal the view of the wheelhouse immediately in front of me, of the compass on its binnacle, of the polished brass Inca ornament of the sun which swayed from side to side with the rolling of the boat and of the windows through which I gazed at the vast expanse of sea.

I had to lend Sam my factor 24 sun lotion because, in spite of his dark hair and eyes, his skin was extremely sensitive to sunlight to the extent that his forehead was blistered and bleeding.

Later, our middle watch showed us a three quarter moon in a "mackerel" night-sky pricked with stars. It was an unforgettable effect always, the light from a clear, un-obstructed moon, the channelled beam of silver that it cast across the ocean toward the boat. On a watch like that there was nothing dark about the night at all. When on middle watch, unless we delayed retiring, we missed seeing the dawn develop fully although the eastern horizon showed us the promise of it before we went to our bunks.

I awoke at 1100 hours to wet decks, ominous sky, and a great, grey, rough sea with white caps and spume, though not so cold. There was not the need to look out for icebergs so much now, but always when on watch, particularly at night, we were on the lookout for such flotsam as the huge containers which sometimes become detached from cargo vessels. These could be dangerously damaging to a boat like ours. We were experiencing favourable winds, judged to be a force 6–7 gale, cracking on at a good pace though a bit swinging to steer. It was beautiful, with dolphins plunging around the bow.

Duff was in the galley and I at the wheel most of the afternoon. For tea Duff served black pudding casserole and mash, with drop scones to follow.

Middle watch a swine – *Helga Maria* was not a happy boat, swinging, bouncing and bumping about all over the place in big, rough seas. Trying to steer east but swinging to the south all the time and got stuck at 190° and would not come round even when the wheel was turned fully to port. I put up the foresail and while I was doing it could feel her come right in the freshening wind – she had been unbalanced, with not enough power for'ard. There was heavy, wetting drizzle most of the watch, feeling chilly with the damp. I wore long johns, long sea socks, trousers, over-trousers, thermal vest, shirt, wool jumper, Barbour weskit and oilskins. Muffled up, toasty warm, but difficult when one needed the loo!

A casual entry in my journal states:

"No engine by the way. Air compression leaked away due to nut vibrated off."

At 0300 hours an increasingly stormy night had necessitated Jack's decision to lower all sails and start the engine, but despite continued attempts, the engine would not start. It appeared that all the compressed air required to kick-start the engine had leaked out of the cylinder. Jack was left with the dilemma of whether to turn back to Newfoundland or crack on for home. He decided upon the latter but battery power was now low and the light over the compass was dim. After our watch I had a couple of drams of Scotch with Duff and, reclining opposite one another on the day bed in the mess, toe to toe, we discussed till daylight our concerns, for engine-less we were power-less, dependent purely on sail and dead reckoning, and completely out of contact with the outside world.

On **Wednesday 12 August** I rose at 1000 hours. I kept trying to heat water for a wash but first Bella came, wanting coffees, and then Jack ditto! I got a wash eventually, just a lick and a promise, as the weather conditions were not conducive to strip washing. We were rattling on at about 7–8 knots through the big, grey, Atlantic swell. Visibility was poor.

We had corn beef hash for tea, tasty, filling and comforting in bleak conditions.

Huw was still very unwell and continuing with his Paracetamol. Duff was not well either, but was nevertheless coping.

The previous day Bella had overheard some conversation between Lynda and me regarding her, Bella's, marked absence from her bunk in our cabin. She was upset that we had talked about her. We had a chat and I hoped things would be OK between us.

This was not an easy part of the voyage. I had not been out of my clothes for several days – too cold to get undressed. It was nigh on impossible to dry any wet clothing and everywhere was draughty, drippy and comfortless – it certainly made thinking of going home seem easier.

During middle watch on Thursday the only way of illuminating the compass was to use a torch – any other task around the boat was accomplished in the dark. Duff and I shared a few medicinal drams afterwards in the mess until 0600 hours, laughing hilariously over memories of rude rugby songs and the like. He was coughing up green phlegm, so, as he apparently had a history of bronchitis and pneumonia, I decided to nip things in the bud and start him on an antibiotic – erythromycin x four per day.

I rose at 1150 hours to a grey, damp, dripping, misty day. We were steering 090° instead of the required 060° because we were losing the wind at 080°. This part of the voyage *could* have got one down. There was a tense atmosphere – I felt uncomfortable now with Jack and Bella.

Duff was glazing a boil-in-the-bag ham, to be served with vegetables for tea.

**Friday 14** – during middle watch Duff was not too well but rising above it. We had a full moon and gale force wind. Duff took down the fore mainsail as we were going too fast. I got to my bunk about 0600 hours.

I was woken at 1000 hours by the excessive rolling of the boat – to be greeted by MONSTROUS seas. I thought, shitting hell! The Atlantic is known for its long deep swell but, by golly, this was more than a swell, with great walls of water towering over the boat. I was immediately reminded of the illustration by Norman Wilkinson, CBE, on the dust jacket of Francis Chichester's book *The Gipsy Moth Circles the World*, which had filled me with apprehension before we left Whitby. The book was still on the shelf by my bunk waiting to be read.

Huw was back on watch, much better but easily tired. Duff was at the helm all afternoon, wrestling to keep the boat on her course of 070° in seas that had been building up all day. Earlier it had been misty and murky but now it had cleared and one could see the whole ocean heaving and rolling, deep yawning troughs stretching between the crest summits. These were awe-inspiring seas, magnificent and unforgettable.

I cooked a big stew, all in one pan, and Duff made pancakes. I forgot to make Bella a veggie meal. Conditions in the galley were very difficult, our arms were tired with hanging on and the decks were hazardously slippery.

Water continued to drip in all over the place, particularly in the for'ard cabin. It was Jack's opinion that while in the hotter climes the timbers of the boat's carvel oak hull had dried, the shrinkage being the cause of her taking on so much water. The bilge was awash. Re-caulking was vital but meanwhile there was nothing for it but to man the bilge pumps continually, round the clock, a punishing regime. Counting the number of my strokes, protected in oilskins and sou'wester, I pumped away as the storm shrieked itself around me in its fury.

At 1145 hours, just as I was getting up from my bunk, in the dark, to go on watch, there was a huge bang, as though we were hit by an express train, and a grievous juddering and jarring of the boat, repeated a few moments later by another of the same, slap-banging the boat over onto her side. I was flung violently forward and then back, painfully wrenching my right shoulder. I was saved from being thrown because I was clutching the edge of my bunk.

There were sounds of loose things rolling about on the decks above me. I scrambled quickly up the companionway and was met by a sort of eerie silence – and a scene of devastation. At first I could see no-one about. Everything was dark, confused, wet and frightening. I could see that planking was stove-in on the port quarter in three places and the rail that held the lashings was ripped away. The lowest step that led into the wheelhouse was gone. Water barrels seemed to be missing, gas cylinders, ripped from their lashings, were loose and swilling about the deck with buckets and other flotsam. Ropes were strewn everywhere. Then Jack was on the scene, talking to Huw at the helm who reported that the *Helga Maria* had been hit by a huge rogue wave on her port quarter, followed almost immediately by another. Twice the boat was knocked right over so that the masts were touching the seas and twice she righted herself. The rest of the crew had now joined us, so it was all hands on deck clearing things up, gathering and securely re-lashing the remaining cylinders, not knowing when another great wave might break over us and wash us away, for the seas were made huge by the furious wind. A night I doubt I could ever forget. During that middle watch of **Saturday 15** – after some semblance of order had been resumed – we all gathered in the wheelhouse. Lynda and I made coffees for everyone, hot, strong and sweet. Jack ordered a tot of whisky for each of us – a most welcome pull-me-round for we were badly shaken.

There continued to be huge seas all night and screaming wind. I was reminded of two lines from my old book *Windjammers*:

> "Must hand and reef and watch and steer
> And bear great wrath of sea and sky."

We tried to get a light to work over the compass. Messed about for quite a while getting new batteries into the yellow (tamper proof) torch. We eventually fixed up a good light with it, although it needed bashing every few minutes to maintain its beam onto the compass. I didn't think there were any more batteries left. I was wet and cold so put on body warmer and oil skins. Someone made up a welcome flask of coffee for Duff and me to have in the wheelhouse. It continued to be a wild night, but thankfully, with no further catastrophes. It was a relief to get into my bunk at 0400 hours. I prayed for quiet seas and safe deliverance. I tried telepathic communication with Rev. Paul Burkitt and thought much about my parents. It was tricky for us, out there in mid Atlantic – without power we had no radio to make a "may day" call and our lifeboat, we discovered, had been washed away by the rogue waves. We were alone out there with very little, apart from what skills we had and our own mental and physical stamina. But how impressed I was and how proud I felt about how calm everyone was that night, just getting on with what had to be done, in appalling conditions. I rose at 1130 hours to big seas but not as big as yesterday. The *Helga Maria* was easier to steer and the watch was uneventful. For tea we ate the remains of yesterday's stew (to which Huw had made additions at lunchtime) accompanied by shredded cabbage, garlic and currants, all served with mashed potato. Duff made banana custard. Jack was starting a cold.

**Sunday 16** and middle watch was wild, wet and cold. We had to reduce sail as we were going too fast and leaning to starboard too much. I steered and Duff got on with the sail work. He got very wet in the net attending to the jib and spent the watch frozen. He did not warm up in his bunk and slept badly. My thermal sleeping bag was waterproof and excellently warm and so it seemed a good idea for him to borrow it for the time being. The afternoon watch was uneventful. I did a mega clear-up in the galley – it was a tip, and so much washing up. It was not possible to carry out my customary chores in there at night because there was no light. It was bad enough trying to make hot drinks with a torch tucked under the arm, attempting to persuade coffee, sugar and milk into the throat of a flask and then to creep cautiously along sea washed, sloping decks to the wheelhouse, dragging oneself in through the door in the teeth of a howling gale – but what bliss when once inside with the door closed – peace and comparative silence interrupted only by appreciative murmurs as the hot restorative liquid slipped down dry throats and cold hands were clasped around hot mugs.

We were getting short of fresh water in the barrels – only one any good as the others had algae or were contaminated with sea water. Duff intended to devise a hand pump, somehow, so we could get water from the main tank. Rationing of water was a must however, as, without a favourable wind, we realised we could be marooned out there for an indeterminate length of time.

The following middle watch was a good one, lit with moon and stars, and with a calmer sea. We were under full sail in a fortuitous wind just then, but much was stacked against us for we had fully absorbed the fact that if there were a case of man overboard, without her engine, the *Helga Maria* could not turn about and carry out a rescue. A sobering thought. As a safety measure Jack released from the stern a long rope with a lifebelt attached, which would be our only chance of survival – if one could grab it – but it would be a very slim chance.

There had always been plenty of opportunity to be private and alone on the boat, allowing the space and time for contemplation. I came then to thinking how, overall, my time at sea was changing me from who I *was* to being an altered person who could never again be quite the same. All experience, of course, is life forming, extreme experience, I decided, formed one extremely – then, it was all about defying the elements and hardships, of sharing those widely diverse situations with my fellows, facing the possibility of drowning, looking beyond that and coming to terms with it, if that was how it must be. It would, after all, be not such a bad death, I thought, compared with decaying into old age.

### We resort to candle light.

It was becoming progressively more and more of a struggle during our middle watches for Duff and me to maintain any form of consistent illumination from the yellow torch with which to light the compass. What light there was had become very dim and was clearly about to expire. We only had candles to fall back on so Duff set a candle within a jam jar. He wrapped the jar in kitchen foil apart from a small window through which a concentrated beam shone. He fashioned a lamp shade for it and the lantern was a big success. As Duff said, "I am amazed at the magnitude of my intellect in creating it!" Yet we only had a meagre supply of candles.

Jack wished to progress as quickly as we might for it was the hurricane season and we needed to be heading as easterly as possible to get into less threatening waters. Of course we were depending now solely on the wind and the ocean current – the former driving us southerly and the latter sweeping us northerly, making it difficult to gauge our progress.

I rose at 1100 hours to a calmer sea and sun. I was at the wheel while Duff fixed up a hand pump in the forepeak to extract fresh water from the main tank. I noticed that the bottom step to the wheelhouse had been partially repaired. For tea we ate curry with dishes of orange, onion and tomato.

Now that Huw was mobile again I could see that he had lost a considerable amount of weight and looked grey and haggard. He was not pulling out of his illness well, which was perhaps not surprising as conditions below decks were desolate – like living in a dripping wet cave.

We were all trying to get as much sleep as we could in order to conserve our energies and, importantly for morale generally, and in spite of challenges in the galley, good filling meals continued to be produced and hot drinks made.

Bella had been feeling the cold badly since leaving Newfoundland. Fortunately I had, in the main, kept very warm, apart from cold feet. I went to my bunk fully clothed, only removing boots, over-trousers and oilskins – it was the best way to preserve body heat. When on watch I wore multiple layers of clothing and I'd been blessed with various wind cheating garments, such as the oil-rig over-trousers.

Jack had not located a foot pump for replacing the compressed air so there was no hope of being able to start the engine. His plan was that, since the first land he anticipated sighting would be the Shetland Isles, when in the lee of the remote island of Foula, twenty five miles west of Shetland, he would send up flares to attract a fishing boat so as to obtain help. Alternatively, if land was not located there as he hoped, he would turn southerly for the Scottish mainland West coast. Importantly we needed to be in as unfrequented waters as possible because of the danger of collision with other craft due to our having no lights for night sailing. It was important to regain engine power at the earliest so that we could make our return to the UK safely, independently with some semblance of dignity!

The following middle watch was most uncomfortable – it was hard to keep balance as we carried out our various tasks as the boat was heaving every which way. The bottom step to the wheelhouse had washed away again.

The afternoon watch was cold but uneventful. We were extra vigilant now on lookout for the Rockall Light and any sign of land so that we could get some idea of where we were. There were large flocks of seabirds bobbing about on the water. Whatever the ocean flung at them they just sat tight, hunkered down in these huge seas, mounting to the crest of a wave, then down the other side into the ensuing chasm, only to float up yet again to the next crest, and so on – just as the *Helga Maria* did, time after time, reassuring me of the boat's construction and capabilities. Do the birds come out here because of the shortage of fish off the Newfoundland coast? (Fishing the Grand Banks was curtailed for at least two years in an attempt to re-stock those famous, once prolific waters. Was it already too late? Who would ever have thought that man's idiocy in over-fishing could have brought things to such a pass?)

We were trying to get a weather forecast on Bella's battery radio and caught the headline news which, from all over the world, was dreadfully distressing. We heard that due to civil war in Somalia there was a country-wide famine. In India there was widespread rioting – Hindus fighting Muslims – leaving over 2,000 dead. Bosnia and Herzegovina becoming independent from Yugoslavia had triggered war between Serbs, Croats and Muslims. At home in the UK unemployment was at a high with 2,700,000 out of work. We felt better off where we were, at sea, but that was not saying much!

On **Tuesday 18 August** the clocks went forward one hour.

Huw announced pleasantly that wearing Lil's tights over his feet and round his neck kept him very warm.

Jack shocked me by saying he could hear all our conversation in the wheelhouse via the connecting speaking tube. That effectively shut me up for the rest of the watch – one wondered what one had been saying!

At that time, while eating our meals at the table in the mess, we had to take care that our plates were not situated beneath the drips from the deck lights above our heads or from the runs of water that followed the beams. As we sat together though, our stomachs replete, we managed to find plenty to laugh about, making light of our gross discomforts. Sam said he was looking forward to landing on Foula and saying, "I'm fresh from Nova Scotia, where are we at?" in his pronounced Canadian accent! He rose from the table, wearing those incredible, baggy oilskin trousers of his, to fill buckets with fresh water from Duff's newly operational forepeak facility, so that we might brew up and relax for a while with mugs of satisfying hot tea. The day bed, where we could sit and relax after a meal, was wet, necessitating oilskin trousers or run the risk of a very wet bottom. The mess was festooned with socks, jumpers, shirts, boots draped everywhere, but nothing was drying. To conserve our fresh water, we were using sea water for washing up as we had done during our four week run towards the Caribbean.

Our watches just then were bitterly cold although, briefly, the glowering grey skies cleared a little to show us a glimmer of sun, and once, to starboard, the arch of a rainbow, only partially obstructed by cloud.

My hair was permanently stiff with salt spray.

During our middle watch on **Thursday 20** we were struggling to steer 060° in the teeth of the north-west wind but managing nearer 030°. At 0400 hours we were glad to hand over to Jack – as he took over the helm he gave Duff and me a bottle of Ballantynes whisky which was a pleasant surprise. It had to be admitted that imbibing a wee dram after a chill and difficult night, to sit and talk and have a laugh and generally relax before retiring to our bunks brought a welcome shaft of pleasure into that very bleak environment. To the extent that Duff one night elected to wear my plaid blanket as a kilt with my over-the-knee fisherman's socks, which was a hilarious sight! He was naturally a very funny man and the laughter he so often caused was a wonderful tonic.

Dead reckoning positioned us approximately 54.4° latitude and 22° longitude, hopefully heading for Rockall, but apparently the light there was damaged, so we might miss it and not get a fix.

Jack lent us for light reading, and in order to cheer us up, *Wrecks on the Shetland Coast*. I felt reassured that his sense of humour was still well to the fore!

For tea we ate cooked mince with onions, garlic, real potatoes, and apple sauce.

Duff and Huw managed to light the oil stove in the for'ard cabin, accompanied initially with clouds of smoke! But none of us were invited in there to get warm. I climbed into my wet bunk with frozen feet and similar spirit. In the mess there were two stoves, but methylated spirit was required to light them – as we had none they were of no use to us. The following night however, after middle watch, I followed Duff and warmed my feet by the stove before going to my bunk and, thus comforted, slept like a log.

We got up to find no lunch – soup cold, and no light under it. I boiled a kettle, made two black coffees and I ate crackers and marmalade. The reason for no lunch this time was that the mainsail boom had swung across and broken its chain, crashing into and breaking the stay. Jack and Bella were making the vital repairs when we got up. Huw had been at the helm when the boat went off course and in coming round the wind had taken the sail and crashed it round, thereby causing the damage. We were lucky, for potentially the mast could have snapped or could have rived up the decking.

It continued to be bitterly cold. We were sailing close-hauled to cope with the persisting northerly winds – south-westerly winds were what we really needed to get home.

Duff made us corn beef fritters (dipped in egg and crushed cornflakes), onions and mash. He looked thin and exhausted. Jack looked tired and harassed, but was keeping up morale by carrying out routine tasks of scraping and varnishing. In fact we all looked battered and sea-worn.

I worked out that we had thirteen main meals left – three cartons of dried mince, four cartons of curry, two cartons of chicken supreme, two cartons of spaghetti bolognese, one tin of strange Chinese food, one tin of corn beef. We shouldn't starve but we had no idea how long we might be out there. We had no fresh vegetables left, apart from onions and potatoes, but we had tinned vegetables remaining.

After tea I was warmed right through, for the first time for many days, by the stove in the for'ard cabin, soothing my injuries of a few days previously – I had fallen on a deck awash with sea water, twisting my right knee and spraining my right ring finger, neither were serious but ached greatly in the cold.

During **Saturday 22** the wind had moderated so that by the time we went on middle watch we were hove to because of the complete lack of it. Duff went below to his bunk for there was nothing aloft to go adrift – all sails were down and lashed. I remained on watch till 0400 hours. It drizzled. A light gusty breeze was just sufficient to move the boom over from time to time, and to moan slightly in the rigging. Otherwise, silence, apart from the occasional eerie sound of a gull. I was scanning the horizon for lights but identified none. I called Jack at 0345 for his watch.

Next day we experienced a warmer day with a stiff wind blowing from the south east which was more what we wanted, but the downside was that the for'ard cabin stove refused to adapt to the new wind direction, blew out and would not re-light.

On **Sunday 23 August** we had a dreadful middle watch of mounting seas and wind to full gale force from the north. I was at the helm and at approximately 0300 hours the compass candle guttered out in a sudden draught and I was left in darkness. I felt about for the torch – there might be a scrap of battery power left – but I couldn't locate it. I whistled for Duff who was scrambling eggs in the galley. Meanwhile the wind took the sails aback and the boat swung round to the north-west – we had the jib, foresail and mainsail up. In very dim torch light Duff relit the candle in the jar and called Jack. We were being swept southerly – we did not want to go that way but had to abide with the wind until we could resume a more north-easterly course. It was exhausting work dropping the sails and setting them all again particularly hard when being hurled about wet decks in a rolling boat. Next morning I was up at 1100 hours to a full gale and enormous seas. We were hove to, with just the fore mainsail set, and riding out the gale so as not to be driven towards a potentially hazardous Irish coastline or to get too far south. The sea anchor was now set astern to help control the wild plunging of the *Helga Maria* through those seas.

**Our gas supply expires.**

Something I had been dreading for some time finally happened – the gas for the galley stove expired.

Throughout our recent hardships our hot teas had been a great spirit-raiser and the thought was grim of not having them to look forward to. Replacement gas bottles had been swept overboard on the night we were knocked over. I had prepared a stew ready to cook, plus a pan of potatoes. Resourceful Duff came to my rescue with a flame gun and boiled the potatoes with that. We managed to make an excellent accompanying salad with tuna, tinned peas, carrots and corn, all tossed with a little vinegar and hard boiled eggs. Future meals however were going to be a challenge.

The ensuing middle watch we were still hove to and I carried out the watch alone with no unpleasant incidents. I was glad to note that the seas were slowly settling.

Rising at 1100 hours I discovered there was no lunch prepared so I had cornflakes and Duff ate nothing. The northerly wind was still blowing us southerly and the sky remained obstinately overcast. We heard over the battery radio that Hurricane Andrew was raging over Florida – would it affect us in any way? We were a sitting target where we were and this filled me with a feeling of helpless dread. We had to get on, but difficult without the right wind. Duff successfully adjusted the jib to stop its horrendous vibration which could be felt throughout the boat.

I could not get in the galley to prepare tea because Bella was repairing the unit top. Later she made a salad but Duff and I had already gone to our respective bunks.

Duff was unwell with earache and a tight chest. I gave him simple linctus as a precaution.

Middle watch on **Tuesday 25** and we were becalmed. It was impossible to gauge how powerfully the Gulf Stream current was sweeping the boat homewards during our battle against the northerly gales. Which, I wondered, was the stronger. Ominously, our candle power to illumine the compass was almost exhausted.

Up to sunshine and a light breeze, steering 020° NE. Jack was hoping ultimately to make it to Stornoway on the Isle of Lewis or to Scalloway in Shetland – oh! please, please, I thought, let's make it to somewhere! Food supplies were getting low, particularly when we were without gas in the galley for cooking purposes. To supply us with some protein we had raw eggs beaten with milk and sugar for lunch, with crackers.

A light in the darkness! – during the afternoon Duff got the paraffin stove going again in the for'ard cabin and it would be possible to cook on the top of it, once it was fitted with a fiddly to prevent the pan flying off. Flasks were filled with boiled water for hot drinks. Duff cooked potatoes and scrambled eggs for tea. We dried out and ate our meal in the glorious comforting warmth, companionably crammed together in the limited space, mostly eating on our laps.

Huw was straightaway put in charge of the heating and cooking in the for'ard cabin. The stove was at the mercy of the wind and sometimes puffed out billows of smoke and went "woomph" and we all leapt a foot in the air!

Duff and I had no more whisky!

**Thursday 27 August** and we were still becalmed so Duff and I split our middle watch, he doing 1200–0200 hours and I 0200–0400.

I rose at 1100 hours to very different conditions – half a gale blowing from the north again, unfortunately driving us south easterly. Struggled with the steering and lost it for a while, veering from 125° – 10°. Duff and Jack tightened up the jib and she came round. I helped Bella on the deck house roof to lash the mainsail. The chain on the mainmast stay was loose because of a broken shackle. I felt a bit vulnerable up there and had to hang on like hell to avoid being jettisoned into the sea.

We ate chicken supreme and macaroni pudding for tea, followed by currant pancakes. All cooked by Lynda and Bella during the afternoon, they having temporarily usurped Huw's role in the for'ard cabin.

The wind came round slightly and was beginning to drive us in a more easterly direction. Every nautical mile we could gain, when the wind enabled us to steer the right course, was mercifully separating us further and further from the dreaded tail end of Hurricane Andrew, the latter being a challenge we could well do without!

Our temperaments were feeling the stresses of wet and cold, the struggle to keep one's balance and carry out even the simplest of tasks during those gales. A conscious effort had to be made sometimes not to snap at one's colleagues about minor irritations – and there were plenty! But, we worked as a team, literally "in the same boat" together, pitting what skills we had, with whatever courage and endurance we possessed, against the elements that flung themselves at our boat as she fought her way homewards.

One afternoon Huw was hurled out of his rocking chair in the for'ard cabin by a gigantic roll of the boat – he hit his forehead hard on one of the cupboard doors and injured his right hand. Luckily he was not knocked out, but was much shaken and took to his bunk. Checking on him later I was relieved to find that he was fortunately suffering no obvious ill effects. Duff became very unwell with a raging sore throat and swollen glands and retired to his bunk.

Middle watch on **Friday 28 August** presented us with stormy seas and near gale force winds. We maintained a course of 100°E. Duff was feeling very poorly, looked hollow eyed, came on watch but soon retired to his bunk with all my throat lozenges. I encountered no problems during my remaining time at the helm.

I was up at 1030 hours to big seas and hail. Later the sun came out and it became warmer in the afternoon. Jack volunteered to do Duff's afternoon watch, but Duff coped well enough despite feeling rough.

Bella and Sam had fallen out – cause unknown. Sam was quiet and withdrawn.

The weather forecast from the battery radio did not seem to tally with where our dead reckoning suggested we might be – further west than we thought? By dead reckoning, if the wind remained the same, we were heading for Barra in the Outer Hebrides.

I could smell my own body and greasy hair and decided to brave the chill temperature in the wash house. I stole a kettle of hot water from the stove and lathered face, hair, ears and neck and felt so much better for it. To complete the improvement I applied deodorant to armpits and donned a clean shirt. It was the first hot water on my person for over a fortnight as I had not been undressing to get into my cold, damp bunk, but I had been regularly brushing my teeth and using the miniature bottles of Listerine the dentist gave me in New York. Such small attentions to one's *toilette* were undeniably morale boosters. Another morale booster was to work alongside as great a person as Lynda – a lady of lovely temperament and always pleasant with everyone. Brave and calm in emergencies. The rest of us were suffering from "been at sea for five months" anomaly, viz. potential shortness of temper, a tendency to hibernate and a lack of motivation to do any job which was not vitally necessary.

The for'ard cabin stove was operating well – Huw would start early to cook tea and then re-heat everything nearer the time. He had a lot to cope with for, with each roll of the boat, a proportion of the contents of the stew pot would slurp over the rim and shoot toward the deck where it was caught in a strategically placed pan and then returned to the pot.

Our range of conversation, when all together after tea, was comprehensive, and, amongst other things one day, we discussed the names for specific quantities of liquid, for example: PIN = four and a half gallons, FIRKIN = nine gallons, BARREL = thirty six gallons, HOGSHEAD = fifty six gallons, PIPE = one hundred and twenty gallons approximately. Completely useless information to us just then but interesting nevertheless! Without the distractions of radio and television conversation on board blossomed. Duff and I one afternoon in the wheelhouse had earnestly discussed, and at great length, the merits, or otherwise, of having a sideboard in one's dining room. This seemingly ridiculous subject dredged up for us numerous childhood and family memories which we were enjoyably able to share.

On **Saturday 29 August** we split our middle watch because we were becalmed again. It was so quiet – just the sound of a sail flapping idly, the sky clear and full of stars and, for a bonus, sight of the northern sky filled with the extraordinary swirling of the Aurora Borealis, the colourful Northern Lights, a phenomenon I had never seen before and which held me spellbound.

Duff introduced an interesting idea – that in the event of our remaining becalmed for any length of time – to try and start the engine using man power, aided by booms, gaffs and pivots to turn the flywheel of the engine to get the pistons going. Otherwise, how long might we continue to wallow there in the waves going nowhere or be blown persistently in the wrong direction? Declining food supplies put pressure on us to forge onwards with all our ability. I felt subdued – worried about a mounting kennel bill for my dog Clem, my casualty job, the lack of land, lack of the right wind, shortage of water now, shortage of coffee, tea and food generally, shortage of drying facilities for clothes. I was frustrated by our helplessness.

Huw was making soup and potatoes for lunch but it was not ready on time for Duff and me. In a biting cold wind I spent some of the afternoon painting the lifebelts in fresh colours (just in case we needed them).

Duff and I made up for the missed lunch by enjoying a hearty meal of curry and rice for tea with pancakes for afters made by Lynda and Bella. Huw had grumbled all day about his role as "stove, hot water and food man", but agreed with Jack to continue. Good, because he was better staying in a warm place to recover completely from his flu type of illness and we really had enough to do on our watches without having to bother making meals. Gales were forecast again.

I noticed that Jack was making ready an anchor rope and chain, and Huw was preparing a lead line. Did they know something I didn't know? Certainly their proceedings induced me to adopt a more sanguine outlook regarding the possibility of the proximity of land. However, during middle watch both Duff and I were quiet and thoughtful – hard to laugh much when we didn't know where the hell we were. At 0330 hours the lantern candle finally expired and we lit a home-made one which Bella had made from stubs. The light from this was so poor that I was unable to read the compass on the binnacle well enough and by mistake I headed far too much to the south and the sails were taken aback. Jack and Lynda came on watch and between us we dropped the sails and reset them.

To contemplate that we would have to heave to each night, due to having no light for the compass, even if there were a favourable wind, was tormenting and ridiculous in the extreme – but *one must be able to see where one is heading!*

Afternoon watch was sunny, no wind, quite pleasant really, but we were going nowhere. I had cold porridge on its own – milk and sugar all gone – followed by carrot and bean soup for lunch.

The bilge continued to be pumped around the clock as we were taking on a lot of water – the for'ard cabin mat was sodden and water gushed in persistently through the oak hull.

**Bizarre behaviour.**

In the main Sam seemed to have been happy enough with us since leaving Canada, but the *Helga Maria* had a way of bringing to light one's inadequacies and I realised he had been finding the going a bit tough of late. He lost control of himself one afternoon, banging and crashing about, kicking things, f... ing and blinding, stripping off on deck and flinging his clothing about (some of which blew away). He was not eating, not dressing warmly enough, had no more cigarettes, appeared to be afraid, in despair and giving in to temper tantrums. He announced he would not do another hand's turn on the f... ing boat and would swim ashore for cigarettes. He refused the offer of a fag from Bella or of a warm jumper from Huw. I felt for him, because I had experienced inadequacies myself, of not being physically strong or knowledgeable enough, but it did no harm to realise that, to find out what one could or could not do, although really, on board, there was no such word as can't – one just strove to do any job, whatever it might be, to the best of one's ability.

Regarding the rest of our crew, from my medical point of view, Bella had a headache, Duff's throat was better and he kept relatively cheerful by messing on with fag ends again for his pipe, Huw was OK, and Jack, well he was giving every sign of actually ENJOYING the challenge of our situation by exuding confidence and good nature. Me? I was all right but had a tearful blip over my soup one day – I couldn't explain to myself why. Our location was such a confused issue – looking at the chart we might well NOT be off the Irish coast heading for Shetland but, because of the powerful northerly gales, being driven more towards the Bay of Biscay or the coasts of France or Spain. We had been sailing completely blind since leaving St. John's and even if we had had a sextant sightings would have been very rare as the sky had been overcast most of the time. Any land fall now would do but with our food supplies becoming critically low time was of the essence.

**Food rationing.**

Huw was now attempting to make one meal stretch into two.

I said to Jack one day that our voyage deserved a book to be written about it – he grinned and said nothing but came to me later and instructed that the name for my book should be "*A Candle for the Atlantic*". I replied that I would have to censor the story a bit but he said "no, tell it as it is". So that is what I am doing.

One afternoon the loo became blocked/full and Huw took it upon himself to deal with it. He was about to tip the contents over the side but, due to the erratic movement of the boat, miscalculated, and the malodorous contents went all over the decks and required much swilling with sea water and brushing to get it all cleared up!

A typical scene in the for'ard cabin at 1750 hours might have been this:

Duff half hanging out of his bunk munching marmalade crackers listening as Huw read out to him excerpts from his book while from time to time rising from his rocking chair to stir the stew or attend to the stove.

Often when I entered the for'ard cabin I would find Huw deeply engrossed in his book.

When I showed interest Huw explained to me that the author was the legendary Bill Tilman, of whom he was a great devotee. This was because of the quality of his writing about exploration and of his descriptions of sailing in a boat, not so very dissimilar to ours, over thousands of miles of the world's oceans. Photographs of Tilman showed a man with a weather beaten face crinkled with smile lines and with a pipe in his mouth.

(Years later, when researching material for this story, I discovered Tilman for myself and became as serious a devotee as Huw had been.)

"Major Harold William (Bill) Tilman was born in 1898.
He served with distinction in both World Wars receiving

the CBE, DSO, MC and bar. He wrote fifteen books on sailing and mountain exploration, considered to be the finest travel books ever written. He was renowned for his Himalayan climbs and sailing voyages. He mostly sailed in Bristol Channel Pilot Cutters and was dependent only on a sextant, a compass, and a short wave radio receiver for shipping forecasts. He carried no life raft and had only very basic rations for his crew. Tilman expected his crew to accept his leadership and judgement without question at all times – he consequently experienced the occasional mutiny along the way! He disappeared in the south Atlantic in 1977 when in his eightieth year."

(The above taken from the introduction to Tilman's eight sailing/ exploration books.)

On August Bank Holiday we were becalmed again and at the start of our middle watch Duff dropped all the sails, lashed them and returned to his bunk. I used the uneventful four hours by bringing my Dictaphone up to date with recent events and then by practising knots – bowline, reef, single and double sheet bend and half hitches. I had in my possession *"A Seaman's Pocket-Book"* dated June 1943 price 1s. 3d. net! Old fashioned though it was it nevertheless held a lot of useful information, including knots. I called Lynda at 0350 hours for her watch and retired to my own bunk.

I was woken early at 0900 hours by a door banging and crashing and by Sam kicking and swearing. He had been sent below by Jack for kicking the wheel while on watch. Sam had also shown a determination not to eat till he got to land! He was now "cocooning" and had taken to his bunk. He was better staying there quietly rather than rampaging around, but he was obviously a concern, we couldn't let him starve to death. I had to enter his cabin later to latch his cupboard doors which were bang, bang, banging with every roll of the boat and getting on everyone's nerves – but he angrily and unreasonably accused me of rummaging amongst his things. Lynda commented ruefully on the "death smell" in his cabin!

The general consensus of opinion at that time was that we would not have been in our present predicament if Jack had only planned ahead properly and made sure that:

a. Navigation aids were well maintained and that he had a second string e.g. a sextant
b. He had a spare cylinder of compressed air
c. He had an adequate supply of gas cylinders
d. He had the boat's generator in working order
e. He had storm lanterns for the various areas on the boat
f. He had a generous supply of candles, and matches with which to light them
g. He had spare batteries for torches
h. There was an emergency food cupboard
i. He had methylated spirit with which to light the stove in the mess saloon.

The afternoon watch was miserably dreary, windy and wet, with no sighting of land, but we saw a land type of bird, like a little sparrow, and a piece of seaweed.

Sam was having repeated outbursts of beating the bulkheads and swearing.

Middle watch on **Tuesday 1 September** gave us big seas and gale conditions. Somehow I overslept and was fifteen minutes late joining Duff in the wheelhouse where I found him and Bella frustrated by attempting to ignite damp book matches, which they managed to do after about four books. This was to light a little paraffin lamp, which Jack had donated to the wheelhouse from his own cabin, because of our total lack of candles and batteries for torches.

Duff was very terse with me for being late and I received the silent treatment. I went into the bow to escape the bad atmosphere, embracing the force of the buffeting wind and rain. I communed a while with my long-dead father, wanting him to know that I understood the love he had had for the sea and boats. Then I spoke into the teeth of the howling gale to my friend, Stephanie, and said, "We are having a difficult and dangerous time but don't worry, I know we will be safe", a sentiment I fully believed. I also chatted companionably to God.

(After I had been home for several weeks, I spent a pleasurable evening with my friend Stephanie, sitting on the floor in front of her cosy log fire and sharing a bottle of wine, when suddenly she said, "While you were away, Rosie, I awoke one night in the early hours. I sat bolt upright because I heard your voice, clear as a bell." She repeated to me the exact words I had spoken to her when we had been in extremis that stormy night. I was utterly amazed, to realise that there had been that transference of my thoughts through the ether and across that wild ocean to my dear friend. Since then I have had a completely open mind, an acceptance and belief in those things for which there is no easy explanation. William Shakespeare knew, as he revealed in his play *Hamlet* with the words *"there are more things in heaven and earth than are dreamed of in your philosophy, Horatio"*.)

Day and night we were pumping the bilge, one hundred times every hour.

During the afternoon watch – after pea soup for lunch – Jack lowered the mainsail because we were going too fast in a north-easterly gale. We were now hove to, riding it out. The *Helga Maria* had had a couple of very hard knocks to her port side from freak waves earlier in the day. I sometimes wondered how Jack felt about the punishment his boat received in those conditions and if he felt it like a personal assault. I certainly felt shock and apprehension as I felt her judder and strain. The boat was rolling, rolling, and Duff and I took cover in the wheelhouse, looking out upon grey skies and great, grey seas. From Tilman's book *Mischief in Patagonia* these words seemed apt:

"I tell you naught for your comfort,
Yea, naught for your desire,
Save that the sky grows darker yet,
And the seas rise higher."

For tea Huw cooked mince and potatoes which we wolfed down. Bella just had potatoes and tomato ketchup. Huw was having problems with the stove again due to downdraught and he was struggling to obtain sufficient heat from it. He was extremely possessive over the stove and all his pots and pans, as he used to be in the galley. I was appalled when he told me that he had had diarrhoea for three days!! I put him on Imodium, fixed up the disinfectant bucket for hand washing and took him off cooking duties for the time being. Sam was a little better, talking and eating but not much of either. He said he hated himself for being a wimp.

## Hunger and Landfall

**Tuesday 2 September** – We were supposed to have arrived in Whitby today – friends and families would be worrying and wondering where we were. The shipping forecast from the battery radio was not good and on middle watch we were hove to, riding out the storm. There was also an announcement from the coast guard for the *Helga Maria* to make contact with them but we did not have the facility for sending radio messages, even if Jack wanted to. Clearly, at home, there were concerns regarding our whereabouts.

We'd adopted peppermint cordial as our hot drink, but when that ran out marmalade water took its place and served as a satisfactory comforter. However, even the supply of marmalade was not infinite and hot water, tomato ketchup and black pepper became the alternative.

Sam, although eating a little, lost control again, was in extremely changeable mood, couldn't tolerate the wheel and would abandon it without warning.

There was still no sight of land during any of our various watches and we were facing big stormy seas and wind. Steering was relatively easy and it was a relief to have the paraffin lamp burning consistently over the compass at night so that we were enabled to stick to our course – but we were still not going in the right direction.

Duff and I were VERY hungry and felt quite light headed at times. For tea we had a big pot of boiled potatoes with a *chow-mein* type sauce and one and a half boiled eggs each. Bella and Lynda contributed un-leavened bread to the meal – we were eating a lot of "stodge" but it helped to fill us up.

Duff's temper was short. He was not getting any rest because of the constant invasion of the for'ard cabin now that it was the only source of cooking facility, warmth and dining area.

Our middle watch was long, cold and uneventful, lightened only by Duff's ridiculous re-arrangement of my woolly hat which had us both laughing! I drank a mug of hot water in the for'ard cabin, then bunk.

Macaroni soup was served at lunchtime with the washings from the mustard pot and tomato ketchup bottle which made, with Duff's damper bread, a filling meal.

During our Thursday afternoon watch we sighted a trawler, approximately two miles distant to port, heading in a southerly direction. Jack chose not to signal the vessel which, in his opinion, was probably Spanish. This left me with a feeling of anti-climax after a surge of hope that we might get help. It was frustrating to watch the trawler so soon lost to sight, but the incident nevertheless briefly gave us a sense of comradeship with other living beings out there in the vastness. She was the first vessel we had seen since leaving St. John's, Newfoundland.

Duff and I were fantasising about food incessantly and when on watch together fondly discussed the merits of sausages, and crusty bread thickly spread with un-salted butter and strawberry jam.

Jack prepared flags, indicating "no power" and "we do not need assistance", to hoist in the event we sighted another vessel.

During the weather forecast on the battery radio there was another plea for Jack to get in touch with Clyde Coastguard.

We saw a pod of pilot whales and continued to scan the sky-line day and night for any sign of land.

**Friday 4 September** – The entries to my journal were becoming a little monotonous, our middle watch presenting us yet again with persistently strong north east wind and big seas. The watches felt long and tedious – the comfort of a mug of strong hot coffee to cheer one's body and soul was but a distant memory. Conversation was sparse due to weariness and tension. Bilge pumping – 136 pumps per hour – was routine. There was leakage of water into the starboard lower bunk in the for'ard cabin, presumably seeping through a gap in the caulking somewhere.

Duff was ravenously hungry all the time and unable to assuage his appetite with our lower protein meals. Porridge and pea soup for lunch and a tea of nine scrambled eggs with cooked potatoes, tinned sweet corn, peas and carrots plus Duff's damper bread, was a typical meal just then which I found hot, tasty and filling.

Duff was angry with Bella on account of her using the galley jug for hair washing.

Sam became more stable but looked fresh out of Belsen. He ruefully admitted that he had been suffering from nicotine withdrawal symptoms and now forcefully vowed to all and sundry that he would never again buy fags, he would not risk repeating the wretchedness of the "cold turkey" symptoms which had been at the seat of his recent behaviours. Huw "had a go" at Bella one day for being a "bloody know all". I'm afraid she had not gained in popularity with us through her becoming so intimate with Jack. Huw was permanently angry with Jack about the imbalance and resentment that had been created on board by his favouritism of Bella.

Huw was, on the whole, of depressed frame of mind just then, given to complaining incessantly to Duff about the poor outlook for us all and about his own personal discomfort.

**Saturday 5** – Middle watch was long, cold and rather silent. I was in a martyred mood, the reason being that, when off watch, I'd not been taking advantage of the comfort of the only warm place on board, feeling that I must rest in the cold, wet mess so as to protect Duff's privacy and sleeping time. It was ridiculous to feel that, particularly as no-one else was following suit, so to hell with it.

There was still absolutely no sign of land or lights and only three days' food left. Two meals a day now were skipper's orders, but that would be no punishment to me since that is all I had had since I came aboard anyway, except when in port. Hunted for food in all the lockers but found none. There was enough food to last us till Wednesday. I breakfasted at 1030 hours on plain boiled rice.

I discovered Jack serenely painting the head buttercup yellow. Pipe in mouth. What a thing to be doing in a crisis somewhere in mid Atlantic! But I found the picture of him doing so strangely reassuring and calming.

Afternoon watch was cold and bright, the wind blowing from the south west for a change. Jack changed onto a starboard tack, the downside of that being that the stove played-up badly again as the cowl couldn't cope with the different wind direction. Duff was inspired and managed to construct, out of a bucket, a cowl protector that he christened "Hamish Grey" to replace the "Charlie

Noble" that had blown away in the Bay of Biscay. The stove burned brilliantly straight away and comfort was restored. So, for tea we had a green soup incorporating peas, olives, macaroni, garlic and pepper – absolutely delicious for our famished stomachs and doubly appreciated after the long struggle with the stove.

A sanguine Bella was preparing a fishing line.

Further gales from the north-east were forecast.

**Sunday 6 September** – Middle watch was very stormy and Jack and I dropped and lashed the mainsail. The cold and wet caused miserable pain in my injured finger end and afterwards I felt a bit sick and had to spend five minutes sitting on the wheelhouse deck. At 0345 hours a light was sighted to port, a light to starboard and, possibly, land looming on the horizon. We were hurtling along at a great pace – Jack lowered the jib and I lashed the billowing sail – had to fling my body over it to hold it down – quite something in the net in a force 8–9 gale. Numb, cold fingers again and got quite wet but I would dry off in my sleeping bag, which I'd reclaimed from Duff. It had been an exciting night but we didn't know yet what land we *might* have sighted, or if there would be a harbour, and if there was, how to get to it without engine power.

I rose next morning to a full force 9 gale and we were hove to. It was raining and visibility was almost zero. When on deck I could scarcely keep my eyes open against the force of the wind. It was disappointing that there was no sight of land.

We had plain boiled rice for breakfast, with no embellishments. Sam took a small amount of rice into his dish and spent ages picking about in it, putting the naturally discoloured grains to one side, very irritating to watch when, in our hunger, we had gobbled ours. He ate what he wanted, got up and abandoned his dish on the table so that it catapulted across the cabin with the roll of the boat and emptied its contents all over the lower bunk and seamen's boxes and into the bilge. Observing this we were aghast at the waste of food – *we* could have eaten that rice. The only time I ever shouted in anger at anyone throughout the voyage was then – I yelled at him because each morsel of food was now so precious that it was possible to fall out over a few grains of rice. Through the for'ard hatch I could see the fore mainsail flapping and angrily suggested to Sam that since it was his watch he should check it out, but he wouldn't.

Huw fell on deck during the morning while helping with the anchors which were slewing about. He suffered no ill effect.

We heard that a force 9 gale was forecast for the Rockall area so maybe that was where we were?

The seas were incredible – the surging crests of the waves were a vivid greenish-turquoise where the light shone through them. As our boat rose to each successive crest she must then descend down, down the other side into the deepest imaginable troughs before she could rise yet again to meet the next crest. It was utterly fascinating to watch how that wonderful boat dealt with the seas – I was lost in admiration for her sea worthiness and had complete faith in her, and her skipper, to get us safely home.

However, a dirtier day would be hard to imagine. The loo kept disconnecting itself from its moorings and freely slithered about the deck. One had to catch it before one could use it.

Duff and I had turned to chewing gum as a pastime – I had found a packet on my bunk shelf. It was acceptable, if for nothing else than it had a sugar coating. I naively thought it might take Duff's mind off the lack of tobacco, but of course it did not, as my journal poignantly described the state he was in:

> "Duff is very short of sleep due to the for'ard cabin being the centre of our universe at present. He is very hungry and very cold. He has no tobacco and is in a dour mood. He sits on the wheelhouse deck, rocking to and fro in

misery. I wish I could help him but there is nothing I can do or say."

**Monday 7 September** brought us heavy rain and a miserably cold day. Jack was changing tack as I went on middle watch and I spent the first hour hauling on and tidying the various halyards. Any conversation between Duff and me in the wheelhouse was centred on food, mainly about the remembered delights of fillet steak and liver casserole.

Light winds were followed by a near gale in the afternoon but to our jubilation we sighted land to starboard – it was a long, dark, but quite definite strip of something that was, at last, not ocean, occasionally disappearing in the sheeting rain. But to our chagrin we were swept beyond it and it was lost to sight in dirty weather. It seemed a bleak looking place. We changed our course and followed a south-easterly direction in an attempt to get back to it. Severe gale force nine was forecast. Our miserable conditions were made all the greater when the stove blew out and would not re-light. We had a cold tea of curry and macaroni. On Jack's orders we were to eat just one meal per day, commencing on the morrow, in order to conserve our remaining food resources. We still had no idea when we might make land fall, being, as we were, at the mercy of gale and current. Sam was eating like a bird and we were all, with the exception perhaps of Jack, looking gaunt.

It was with great relief that we re-sighted the land mass at 1900 hours and we were now closer to it and could discern that it had immensely high rocky cliffs. I privately wondered if it could be St. Kilda. It was certainly not Shetland, but where?

Middle watch of **Tuesday 8 September** I worked on my own because we were hove to. During the night I sighted, very clearly, a flashing light to starboard. There were three flashes followed by a seven second interval, followed by three flashes and so on. The four hours went quite quickly really – came up to date with my

Dictaphone, attended to the bilge and checked that we were not drifting dangerously. I handed over to Lynda at 0400 hours. Woke at 0900 hours but stayed in my bunk till 1015 hours because I was not expecting any breakfast. However, there was some curry, macaroni and rice mixture left over so I jolly well ate it and had a drink of hot water.

On watch in the afternoon it was hard work steering. We were following an unfamiliar, dark, dramatic coastline of immensely high cliffs with waterfalls tumbling down them, their spume blown southerly by the gale in swirling spindrift. We were looking for signs of human habitation. We spotted an aerial mast and a small community in one small fjord, but we were swept past it. Further on a signal station – we passed that too. Then the weather closed in. Duff was in the crow's nest – he and Jack were looking for a possible safe berth for the night.

To the left of yet another great waterfall cascading down those dark, immensely high cliffs was the entry to another fjord. This time the wind obliged, enabling us gradually to approach and ultimately turn into its mouth. Ahead, through the mist and gloom and at some distance to starboard where the fjord opened out, we could make out a green roofed white church and little village.

# 24

## Safe Haven in the Faroe Islands

The moment we entered the fjord we lost the wind because of the height of the menacing cliffs on either side. It seemed the strangest contrast to what we had been experiencing out at sea, but we were now becalmed! After taking stock of our present plight it was clear that we were going to need assistance and accordingly Jack gave a long blast on the horn so as to alert the village of our presence. We waited in hope, but despite the loud boom echoing around the bay there was no visible response from the village. Jack and Huw searched for and discovered the *Helga Maria's* stash of distress flares and let one off but although in the misty gloom the entire sky seemed illumined by the weird light of the flare, disappointingly there was again no response. There was nothing for it but to try once more and a second flare was ignited – and at that moment a powerful-looking fishing trawler churned into the fjord from the open sea, and, seeing us, slowed and came alongside.

Jack shouted across to the skipper to explain our lack of power and the skipper shouted back, "We take you in." Upon enquiry we were astonished to discover that we were in the Faroe Islands, so very far north of where we had expected to be.

Consulting the chart in the wheelhouse I shook my head in semi-disbelief when I realised how incredibly powerful the Gulf Stream current had proved itself to be, hurling us ever forward to reach this haven despite the constant northerly gales our boat had fought. It felt like a miracle, because the next stop would have been Finland or the Arctic and our food supply would not have lasted. Unknowingly we had been swept well clear of the west coasts of Ireland, of the Outer Hebrides and the Shetland Islands to this, the east coast of Eysturoy (bird island) which is one of the most northerly regions of the Faroes.

We dropped all sails and lashed them. While Jack and Duff remained aboard to superintend the short tow to Fuglafjørður, the rest of us were invited onto the trawler. We were taken below to a dining room where the aroma of coffee simmering in percolators and the vision of sideboards laden with smorgasbord inclined us to think that we were dreaming! With shock and delight we gradually assimilated the luxurious accommodation of this Faroese trawler. We were invited to help ourselves and we needed no second bidding. Arranging ourselves gratefully around one of the tables we satisfied our hungry stomachs with a fantastic meal of cold meats – and fish, and bread, and tomatoes, and spare ribs and salad... It was so good to drink coffee again. It was so good to feel safe again – hard to take in really, and all in the immaculate, modern, well equipped and cosy ambience. If that were not enough we were invited to use the showers (I wonder why!). When I stripped off I did not recognise my own body – I wondered where my breasts had gone but they seemed to have been replaced by muscle! I was very thin.

From the wheelhouse of the trawler we were able to phone home in order to put the minds of friends and relatives at rest. I tried to contact my daughter, Sally, but she was not in. Then I phoned my friend Stephanie to let her know that I was safe and for her to let the hospital know too. It was such a relief to be able to do that.

On our way back to the *Helga Maria*, now safely berthed in the harbour of Fuglafjørður, we could see that the village was perched on the edge of the bay, expanding slightly into the surrounding steep hills. Its economy, we heard, was fish processing and the production of fish meal. Before we could get back aboard we were surprised to be interviewed by a Faroese Television crew. Duff, who had joined us by now, gave them the information they needed. He and I went for a walk afterwards. I got to my bunk at 0200 hours.

When I arose the following morning it was after a sleepless night, probably due to the novelty of being safely in port, or the unfamiliarity of a relatively motionless boat, perhaps the anticipation of exploring our new surroundings. I scrambled up on deck to find a dreary wet morning. TV and press people were all around the quayside. What a surprise to realise how much interest we had aroused! I was interviewed even before my breakfast of coffee, brown bread and honey aboard the trawler. A question I was asked during my interview was, "What is a lady like you doing aboard a boat like this?" I can't remember what my reply was.

I received a message to phone Sally. I did so, on a two-way phone, as the press wished to record the call.

A cylinder of compressed air was brought aboard and Lynda and I re-provisioned at the local supermarket. The electrician who came and checked our system very generously brought for us a large salmon and some frozen fillets of white fish, Duff was in a thundering bad mood all day.

Jack spent time with the captain of our tow vessel, extending warmest thanks for his assistance and hospitality. He then informed us that next day we were to head for Torshavn, to a new berth there.

Accordingly at 1700 hours on the morrow we departed from Fuglafjørður under engine power – oh, engine, heart beat of our boat, welcome back! We enjoyed fantastic views as we headed for the open sea and Torshavn, the latter being located on the southern part of the east coast. It is the capital and largest city in the Faroe Islands

171

and would be a more suitable launching pad for our departure homewards. It was a bitterly cold afternoon.

We ate an afternoon tea of cheese, brown bread, margarine and strawberry jam – what luxury! However, the last two days of plentiful food had certainly overloaded my digestive system. I had been feeling extremely fit on the plain tack, although I was very, very thin and I don't know how well we would have fared for a longer period with so little protein. There were probably enough nutrients for a small female but not enough for a big man doing heavier manual work – although, of course, we had all shared the same sort of work and we had all experienced the same degrees of wet and cold.

We got into Torshavn at 2310 hours and berthed near the fish dock. We all had mugs of tea and, feeling very tired due to not sleeping the previous night, I was glad to hit my bunk.

The next morning I was up at 0745 hours, woke Duff, put the kettle on and we both partook of a breakfast of hard boiled eggs and brown bread before setting out in pouring rain to procure ice in order to keep the gifts of fish chilled. We got it all put away in a big cold box. Upon enquiry we learned from the locals that this modern harbour was built in 1927. During the morning, while gas cylinders were being brought aboard, a reporter arrived representing Tyne Tees television, namely Andy Kluz, a past acquaintance of Edna Whelan's. He had interviewed her the previous year regarding Jack's voyage to Jan Mayen Island. He brought with him rum and whisky and we enjoyed a most convivial afternoon. In the evening Huw, Duff and I were invited to his hotel where we ate an excellent cold meal of prawns, ham, rare beef and salad plus two bottles of wine.

It rained all of the following morning while the press and TV people interviewed and filmed us prior to our re-location from the fish dock to a more suitable berth. Meanwhile the galley was back in use again, and we prepared, for lunch, a feast of baked salmon with potatoes and peas.

We were made aware of certain facilities at the local Rowing Club, so during the afternoon Huw and I chose to try these out and had the luxury of a welcome shower, sauna and swim. In the evening, with the exception of Huw and Duff, who went to bed early, the rest of us, including the harbourmaster and Tyne Tees TV Andy, accepted the invitation to visit the home of Knut and his wife, local residents, for a meal. We arrived at 1900 hours, initially being ushered into a small hallway where we gathered in a circle as a goblet of Schnapps was passed round. We each took a swig from the shared receptacle, our host then blessing the house and those within. This was a local custom and I thought it created a wonderful welcome. We progressed up a small stairway into a spacious open plan living/dining area which was so warm and comfortable that I nodded off briefly! We were served with a meal comprising fish soup, followed by a main course of whale meat, whale blubber, dried fish and a great tureen of potatoes and vegetables. I at first looked askance at the great thick chunk of blubber on my plate, with its daunting black rind. However, when sampled, I discovered how delicious it was, with what I would describe as a subtle sweetness to the crispy fat. We drank beer, interspersed with spirits served in a small goblet and knocked back in one. During the evening we were joined by a delightful couple who sang and played the guitar.

It was a complete joy and a privilege to be included in that company, receiving such warm, never-to-be-forgotten hospitality. We returned to the boat at 0100 hours.

The generosity shown to us continued when the following day the harbourmaster insisted on buying us more groceries, and during the day various visitors came bearing gifts of mussels, huge cod and flat fish. From a near starvation state we now had food coming out of our ears, thanks to these good people.

During conversation with some of the fishermen we heard about the annual slaughter of pilot whales which was legally carried out there, and at one other township in the islands. It is a long established ritual where scores of pilot whales are driven towards the beaches and are slaughtered. They provide the islanders with a beneficial and nourishing food source. We were led to believe that osteoarthritis was almost unknown in these islands, thought to be due to a diet based around this creature. Jack and I though felt horrified by the descriptions of the slaughter and the sea turned red with their blood. We hoped that there were at least still plentiful numbers of them in the ocean to sustain their population.

Further gales were forecast, preventing us from setting sail, so Lynda, Bella and I went for showers at the Rowing Club in the morning, followed by a salmon lunch for us all on board. Later, tea was a meal of white fish and fried potatoes.

My journal relates my thoughts on how things were just then:

"Duff has completely withdrawn from me, not speaking to me at all. I miss his friendship. The voyage is ending in complete disharmony between the various factions. Lynda, Huw and Duff are upset by Jack's relationship with Bella. But why should that mar Duff's friendship with me? I expect he is just tired of me now after five months – best finding out about it now. I suppose we may all go our separate ways when this is over and only rarely meet, if ever. I have arranged to keep in touch, however, with Lynda, she is such a sane person."

**Sunday 13 September** dawned and a huge breakfast was served of fish cakes, herrings, fried eggs and coffee, but eggs, bread and coffee were enough for me. The forecast was favourable so we left Torshavn at 0900 hours, taking to the ocean under engine power and sail, heading for Scalloway in Shetland. It felt SO good to be back at sea again but it was a sadness to leave behind the excellently kind people we had met during our stay in the Faroes.

Clem dog, here I come, I mused, and as I thought of him my heart lifted as I remembered the quirky nature of that eccentric Irish canine.

# 25

## Heading for Shetland

During the afternoon watch Duff was very terse and said he was going to leave the boat in Scalloway, that he might as well be destitute there as anywhere else. The man was clearly very depressed. When he had arrived in Whitby a couple of years previously the circumstances were that he had simply walked away from apparently irreconcilable difficulties. He wanted an escape and he found it in Whitby, with Jack and the boat. Without them, he *would* be destitute, until he found an alternative. I felt distraught for him. I cooked a tea of fish, cauliflower and potatoes followed by apples, cake and a pot of tea.

Middle watch was a nightmare – Sam neglectfully did not call me till after midnight so inevitably Duff was cross because I was late on watch. Then he was cross that the previous watch had not set the sails properly (the jib and foresail were flapping wildly) and then I did not hear him correctly when he shouted to me to lower both fore sails – I thought he meant only one. We did not speak to one another again apart from my saying that it was a shame that our friendship should end in a morose silence.

I rose at 1030 hours, had a good wash, deodorised, put on clean

176

clothes and felt as good as new. A lunch of sausage and mash was not ready for Duff and me going on watch, but I took him a mug of coffee in the wheelhouse, which he accepted. We talked a bit, but it was all about how bitter he felt as a result of Jack's attitude toward him throughout the voyage, about the detrimental effect of Jack's and Bella's relationship, particularly as Jack was against couples on board in the first place (and why Duff and I had remained "just good friends" and not even that a lot of the time) and how he would be destitute when he went ashore. I sought to find a way of turning the negative thinking toward a more wholesome outlook. I would have so preferred that he could have felt more positive regarding his experience of the voyage, to have put the bad times down to experience, to have learnt by his mistakes, as we all had had to do. He was so hurt when Jack asked anyone else to help with the tea time meal, considered it a slight, such as the day when Jack suggested that Lynda prepare the halibut for tea. Duff was irritated, too, that Sam was belatedly taking forever to wash up the lunch things. He petulantly steered clear of the galley completely, leaving Lynda to put the fish in a skillet and setting it to bake. Duff would then not help me to put finishing touches to the meal and said he would not eat it. He had not eaten lunch because of its being late. He was looking skeletal and stressed, was mentally in a bad way and a problem for everyone to cope with, particularly me, who was grunter in the middle.

The awkward motion of the boat was making it hell in the galley, the oven door kept flying open every few minutes and it was hard to keep one's balance. I made a salad with rice, orange, apple, carrot, green pepper and hard-boiled egg, also put marinated herring on a plate with bread and butter, all to accompany the baked halibut.

We were traversing the Faroe/Shetland Channel. It can be a treacherous stretch of water so we were hurrying across it as best we could but were only achieving about three knots due to fighting head-on waves.

# 26

## Shetland

On **Tuesday 15 September** at 0600 hours, in the rain, we cruised into Scalloway harbour on the west coast of Shetland. Jack spoke with the harbourmaster who directed us to a slipway where the process of caulking the *Helga Maria*'s leaky hull could at last be commenced.

After supermarket shopping and arranging for the supplies to be delivered to the boat, Lynda, Sam and I caught a bus to Lerwick where I bought a Shetland jumper and some booklets about the locality. Having missed the last bus at 1700 hours we took a taxi back to the harbour. We ate halibut for tea, cooked by Bella. We utilised the showers at the Yacht Club and later visited the Scalloway Hotel where we were able to unwind at last, have a few beers and startle the locals by dancing to the music on the juke box. But I felt un-earthly strange and lost.

On Wednesday Jack was interviewed by a young man from the local radio station. Everyone else went ashore and travelled their separate ways. I walked along the ridge of the hill overlooking Scalloway, soaking up the beautiful views from there and afterwards visited the little museum. Huw and Lynda went to the bank at

Lerwick so that Huw could withdraw cash to pay for the *Helga Maria*'s caulking and repairs.

Quite late that evening Duff and I were invited by a young man, whom we had met at the hotel, to his home for drinks, music and, as it turned out, for marijuana. It was not possible to converse with anyone sensibly at this gathering but the atmosphere was most pleasantly relaxed and smiling as guests lounged on floor cushions in the candle-lit rooms. As a non-smoker I did not partake, although it seemed to me that I inhaled enough anyway, from the general atmosphere, to render me very mellow, a state I enjoyed until well after I returned to the boat in the early hours!

For a couple of days we all worked hard on the boat's hull by using a high pressure spray gun to clear weed, by applying anti-foul, re-caulking where necessary and painting. In the evenings after tea we revisited the hotel bar where enjoyably we mingled with the locals. A perceptive and interesting man named Fraser said he thought Duff would destroy me "because he is a woman hater". Certainly Duff had continued to cut himself off from me to a very great extent and was being morose and withdrawn. However, there was plenty of highly convivial company around and after a beer or two I found I was well able to relax and enjoy myself with the rest of the crew. New friends that we made returned to the boat with us and we would talk till very late.

The following afternoon – after breakfasting on porridge and eggs and being idle for much of the morning – Duff and I meandered around the town to see what was on offer. In a charity shop I bought a pair of extra-small-size trousers because the ones I was wearing were falling off me due to my weight loss. As we wandered around we met an extremely kind lady called Debra who treated us to afternoon tea in a gem of a little tea-and-coffee shop. She was fascinated by our tales of the voyage. Wherever we went we met wonderful, generous, hospitable people.

Huw was not well and stayed in his bunk all day.

Frustratingly, the *Helga Maria's* engine would not start due to problems with the compressed air again. The day's forecast was for south-easterly gales, subsiding by nightfall. There was no sign yet of Jack repaying me any of the money I lent him so I had frantically to search in all my pockets in order to find the wherewithal with which to go out.

I was feeling disturbed, unsettled and confused regarding Duff's and my friendship and decided to be straight with him and confront him with my feelings that, as we were so nearly home, all should be made clear between us, that it was obvious to me that he was gradually phasing me out of his life and that I consequently freed him of any ties or obligations to me. That seemed to hurt him and he told me to stop saying such things.

On **Sunday 20 September**, Bella, Lynda, Jack and I walked through the mist along the coast line ending up at the Yacht Club for a drink before lunch. We ate our chicken tea there too, cooked by Lynda and me, and afterwards we sat and watched a Harrison Ford and Melanie Griffith film *Working Girl* on TV. It made a nice change and I was in bed by 1030 hours. I slept badly though, and had palpitations – I seemed to be in a mess, in limbo.

On Monday Jack phoned Grimsby and ordered starting equipment for the engine.

Sadly Huw was not at all well and decided to go home – he'd had enough of waiting around there in Shetland with little to do and was desperate to return to the comfort of home and his dear Lil. So the ferry took him over to the mainland and he would continue his journey by train. He seemed old and battered as he left but I knew he took with him a sense of fulfilment at having achieved the voyage. It had long been his ambition to sail the seas in a relatively small craft, having spent the war years in large ships, and at last he had done so. I would miss him very much, a benign, wise man, always warm and kind to me and I knew I would keep in touch with him and Lil when I returned home.

I was feeling aimless, "chewed up" and a spare part – something to do with my having experienced over the last five months a life at full tilt, fully employed, and I was not adapting well now to feeling unemployed, as it were. The watches we had worked had made a framework for our days and without them I felt adrift. I read a book in the for'ard cabin for a while. In the afternoon Duff and I went to Lerwick to pick up the engine starters and he was able to draw some money from the bank to which, apparently, he was due. We enjoyed a walk and visited the museum there. I fell asleep in the bus on the way back. We ate cold lamb and vegetables for tea.

Next morning a big air compression machine was brought to the quayside and after much time and care (the connector was not perfect for the purpose) our cylinder was filled. So, with air, water and food aboard an attempt was made to start the engine – at first she only operated on one cylinder, but then two and began to sound like her old self again with that reassuring throb-throb-throbbing that was going to take us back to our home port.

I phoned Stephanie to let her know we were leaving Shetland. We all of us, except Sam, had a few drinks at the Scalloway Hotel to say goodbye to our many new-found friends. I was glad to have some beers inside because of mixed feelings regarding this last part of our travels.

At 1700 hours we pulled away from the quayside into the rain and the overcast afternoon. Soon we passed Foula, well away to starboard. It felt, yet again, so good to be back at sea, back in our routine, but now with one man down.

Alone on watch I contemplated upon how the relative simplicity of life aboard the *Helga Maria* had suited me so well – an uncluttered world where I learned the role I was to play and just got on with it, dealing with the vagaries of wind and weather and disparate personalities as I'd gone along. The voyage for me had been mind-blowing. It had been a life-altering education into what was really important in life – which was not the need for material things for I realised how little I had needed during the last six months, in fact just the few items I had packed on the shelf around my bunk, but rather about the purity of sharing and thankfulness, appreciation for what we had, however little. I made a vow never to waste food, having experienced real hunger first hand, and indeed never to waste anything if I could avoid it.

For tea we had haddock, broccoli and potatoes. Duff went to his bunk and did not eat, but he seemed, nevertheless, a much happier man now he had his own money in his pocket.

Our middle watch was uneventful. Various boat lights were visible. We continued with hourly bilge pumping (200 pumps at a time in spite of the re-caulking.). Duff was chatty and pleasant and after our watch we shared the best part of a bottle of his rum. This was excellently relaxing and I toppled into my bunk at 0600 hours, sleeping like a log till 1130 hours. Painting parts of the boat continued during the afternoon. I prepared eight haddock for tea – they were a gift from the Shetland fishermen – but they smelt unpleasant and I could not face eating them. I felt very tired – most unusual for me – and retired to my bunk.

**Friday 25 September** – Our middle watch was a dramatic one. We were off the Aberdeenshire coast when over our freshly charged radio we heard a distress call from a de-masted German yacht. The Aberdeen Coastguard and Lifeboat had been alerted. Jack made the offer to help and stand by, and we altered course slightly to the west to locate the injured vessel. We were able to lead the lifeboat to the scene because they could see our radar signal very strongly whilst that of the yacht was weak. We ultimately left the area knowing that the rescue was now in the skilled hands of the lifeboat crew and we continued on our way. Jack and Bella had come on deck and lowered our sails as there was quite a swell running. The four of us had a delicious fry-up of mealy pudding and fruit dumpling and after a couple of tots of rum with Duff I hit my bunk.

I was still getting thinner and thinner, looking battered and sea-worn, and my hair needed washing. I would have to pull my socks up for the return to Whitby, the latter event making me feel panicky for some reason.

The afternoon watch I spent washing up, pumping the bilge and painting the *Helga Maria* sign on the ladder against the mast. The last half hour of the watch I was at the wheel – the sea was like a mill pond, the air mild, with gannets, puffins and seals in evidence. We were not far off the Northumberland coast. Bella, Lynda and Sam were painting too, the boat's appearance benefitting from the attention. We ate steak and vegetables for tea.

On **Saturday 26 September** during our middle watch the *Helga Maria* entered the harbour at North Shields on the Northumberland coast, completely unannounced, at approximately 0300 hours. There was just Jack, Duff and me to see her safely in. After she was tied up Duff and I went for a stroll in the pouring rain along the quayside to see the alterations and improvements which had apparently been carried out recently. After which the best plan seemed to be to devour a bowl of muesli and retire to my bunk.

At 0845 hours Andy Kluz of Tyne Tees TV came aboard.

Now, at this point in my story, entries into my journal ceased, and so the rest of this narrative is purely from memory.

# 27

## Our return to Whitby

It was **Sunday 27 September** and thick fog delayed our departure from North Shields and our heading down the east coast, so it was early evening before we made the final run. As we neared Whitby, to our amazement, we noticed that a flotilla of assorted vessels was following the *Helga Maria* now, to her port and to her starboard, and astern of her, accompanying her as she approached her home port and welcoming her with a cacophony of sounding horns. The Whitby lifeboat let off a maroon.

We were all on deck, Jack at the helm. We had rigged the boat with flags from many nations and these gave her a suitably festive appearance. Through mist and dusk we glimpsed at last the beckoning lights of Whitby harbour, the Haven under the Hill. It was, with almost disbelief but with seething excitement, that I saw how the east side of the harbour below the abbey was thronged with bounteous crowds of people, as was the entire length of the quayside, and there were banners and clapping and shouts of "welcome home" and we were waving back and feeling so touched, amazed and grateful to everyone for having turned out to greet us in such a way. Right on the very edge of the quay, nearest to where our boat would come to rest, wearing a bright pink sweat shirt and jumping up and down in excitement, was my friend Stephanie. As soon as we were tied up I climbed the iron rungs onto the quay and amidst the milling throng she and I hugged, and it felt just grand to be back.

Edna greeted us joyfully and with a gift for each – a navy sweat shirt with the logo *Helga Maria* across the front – a fitting souvenir of our journey. It was so kind and thoughtful of her to have procured them for us.

Jack had remained on deck and was looking up and laughing and joking with those on the quay. Someone shouted, "What are you going to do now Jack?" and he replied, "Enjoy a hot bath and have a party."

Stephanie left me to fetch my car. I gathered my belongings and packed them into my sleeping bag and emotionally bade *adieu* to bunk and boat and clambered ashore again.

I don't think any one of us wanted to go home just yet – we were on a high, still slung together by an invisible umbilical cord and anyway we were being pressed into meeting up at the Elsinore where a "welcome back" celebration was in progress. So, in the misty dark we left the harbour behind, crossed the road and wound our way up steep Flowergate until we reached the pub, festooned as it was with flags, bunting and banners. Once within that warm, bright place, alongside crew, dear friends and well wishers, a party we certainly had, and it seemed such a highly appropriate course of action, as that was, after all, where my story had really begun.

# Epilogue

Most of that evening passed in a blur of conviviality. Jack and Bella joined us. I overheard Jack tell a friend that the women throughout the voyage had been by far the strongest, both mentally and in general stamina. I couldn't help feeling a little rush of pride for us "girls".

Guy Reed, whom we had last seen in Mystic Sea Port, Massachusetts, walked into the bar having driven over from the Yorkshire Wolds when he heard our boat was in. It was wonderful to see his great broad smile and hear his voice again.

Lynda was persuaded early on in the evening to return home to Hawsker with her family who had met her on the quayside. They were eager to have her back in the fold!

Sam at this point had no idea where he would spend the night or spend the next few days until he was ready to set out and explore further afield in the UK. Duff's future movements were also most uncertain – so when I offered accommodation at my house, which was only twelve minutes' drive away, it was readily accepted by them both. Guy asked if he could come too since he did not want to face the drive back to his parents' home that night. So it was that when we eventually chose to abandon the party we packed my vehicle up to the gunwales with baggage, and with half the crew of the *Helga Maria* aboard I set out on the short drive home. The time I had dreaded, of our complete

186

disbandment, the abrupt end of all we had shared, was, for the time being, postponed.

The following days were pleasantly busy. I retrieved my dog from the boarding kennels. I collected my canary. We provisioned. We de-briefed. I learned that I was not expected back at work for a couple of weeks. Stephanie came round and commented on how glad I must have been to luxuriate in my deep Victorian bath after all those weeks of hardship – but in fact I had been unwilling to wash away the last of salt from skin and hair and thereby lose that last, now so fragile, link with the sea!

Sam ultimately set out on his travels and disappeared from my ken. Guy went home to the Yorkshire Wolds.

I returned to work and at first found it hard to be indoors all day, to wear my formal nurse's uniform. It was hard to contain the strength I had developed in my arms and shoulders, built by hauling on halyards and pumping bilges, and in my legs when balancing myself on heaving decks. Whenever the opportunity arose I escaped into the yard outside the department to flex my muscles and fill my lungs with fresh air. But it was good to be back amongst my colleagues and to continue the work I enjoyed so much.

I wasn't sure what Duff would do, but he stayed, as I had so much hoped. We settled into a form of life together but he was unwilling to return the feelings I had for him in the way I so badly longed for. There was too much of himself that he held back, things that he chose to keep hidden from me, a darkness that ate and ate its destructive way, always that impenetrable wall between us. It could not go on. After three years he left one night and never returned.

That wonderful character and gentleman, Huw, gave highly entertaining and graphic talks about the voyage to various groups and societies when he got home. He died in October 1998 in the 60th year of his marriage to Lil. Lil has given me access to journal notes that Huw made during the voyage and these have been most interesting for me to read. Lynda, with her husband David, lives close to Whitby still. She has helped me with certain aspects of this story and has written a poem for this book.

Guy lives now with his wife and family in Hertfordshire. He has loaned me fifteen hours-worth of video that he filmed, up to his leaving the boat in Mystic, Massachusetts.

Edna Whelan died at the grand age of 95 in June 2015 Duff, Sam, Bella and Fingers have proved to be untraceable and necessarily their real names have been changed.

Mystery surrounds the end of the *Helga Maria*. I'm not entirely sure when it was that she was no longer to be seen in the harbour but I moved to Scotland and it was not until much later, when I heard of Jack's death, that I enquired about her whereabouts and was told that Jack had attempted to sell her in Denmark, place of her birth. That seemed appropriate but later it came to my ears that he had failed to sell her and that the Danish harbourmaster had not wanted what he termed a "scruffy old boat" on his quayside any longer and that in desperation Jack had taken her out to sea and scuttled her. I could not grasp that he would do such a thing and the thought saddened me greatly and conjured up for me the vivid image of that burnished-brass Inca ornament of the sun, the one that hung on the bulkhead in the wheelhouse above the binnacle, that had swayed rhythmically to and fro with the rolling of the boat and had been part of my vision during each of the countless times I had stood at the helm. But now I imagined it finally engulfed by the flood waters as the boat sank beneath the waves.

But later again, however, I learned from Peter, Jack's son, that as far as he knew the boat had indeed been sold in Esbjerg, Denmark, as a sail-training vessel. Mysteriously though her name plates from around her bow, *Helga Maria,* had been discovered somewhere on the Danish coast, washed up by the sea.

Maybe one day I will have the truth confirmed about what happened to that truly wholesome boat. For me, Whitby harbour is much the poorer for the lack of her unique presence. Meanwhile, I say with all sincerity and from the bottom of my heart, "God bless her", wherever she is.

# Quiet Musings

by Lynda Jackson

On her voyage across the North Atlantic from St. John's, Newfoundland to the Faroes, Shetland and home to Whitby aboard the *Helga Maria*.

Hey-ho Jack m'lad
Saw us through both good and bad,
Adventurous spirit, a tot of rum
A great forerunner of things to come?
A Danish seine-netter, two-masted, sturdy and strong,
built for fishing in times long gone.
A dedicated crew, stout-hearted and keen
(not a trace of "motley" to be seen).
Wind in her sail stretching braces
see the smile on crew's faces.
Black nights, bright stars, slowly emerging sunrise.
Gale force winds, giant waves looming, rain and squall,
timbers creaking – she took them all.
Turquoise whirlpools after the storm,
phosphorescence sparkle greeting the dawn.
Riding the swell on still, windless days,
drifting slowly through the haze.

Quiet frustrations under the skin,
not to worry we will win.
Compass lit by candle glow,
Watch it flickering in the breeze.
Guess that would be the hardest watch to handle
"Mind you don't sneeze!"
Tinned peas with pancakes was the fare,
each scrap eaten with hungry care.
Gannets and terns wheeling, swooping,
powerful wing tips just tracing the ocean,
Some resting and floating, in tune with the motion.
Sunsets brooding, icebergs and whales,
splendid dolphins playing to the fore.
Could we honestly have asked for anything more?

# Glossary

Aft... the rear of the boat.

Barque... a three-four-or five-masted sailing vessel, square rigged, but with fore and aft sails on the mast farthest aft.

Barquentine... a three-four-or five masted sailing vessel having square sails on the foremast only.

Beam... the greatest width of a boat.

Bilge... waste water which collects in the bottom of a boat.

Boom... the spar which extends from the mast to which the foot of the mainsail is attached.

Bosun, bos'n, boatswain... a highly skilled crewman in charge of sails, rigging, anchors, cables and all deck work.

Bosun's chair... a device used to suspend a person from a rope to perform work aloft, often a simple plank.

Bow... the front of a boat.

Bowsprit... a spar that extends forward from the bow.

Brig... a two-masted sailing vessel having square sails on both masts and a gaff mainsail.

Bulkheads... partitions within a ship's hull or superstructure.

Bulwarks... sides of a vessel above deck level.

Carrack... an armed merchant vessel formerly used by Spaniards and Portuguese.

Carvel-built... built with planks flush at the seams.

Caulking... filling a seam or joint on a ship's hull with tow, oakum and pitch to make watertight.

Close-hauled... spars supporting sails braced up tight so as to sail close to the wind.

Companionway... a staircase leading from the deck to cabins and saloon below.

Draught... depth of water displaced by a ship.

Fjord... a long, narrow, steep-sided inlet into the sea coast.

For'ard... at the bow (forward).

Gimbals... a double concentric metal suspension fitting for supporting nautical instruments in a horizontal position.

Halyard... rope used to raise or lower a sail.

Heave-to... bring a boat to a standstill.

Jib... the foremost triangular sail set over the bowsprit.

Knots... units of a boat's speed, one nautical mile per hour.

Keel... a boat's lowest timbers, running from stem to stern, upon which the boat is built.

Lead, lead-line... lump of lead on the end of a line dropped over the side of a boat to test water depth.

Maroon... a loudly detonating signal rocket.

Port... left side of a boat.

Prow... the bow of a boat.

Purse seine netting... a method of fishing that employs a seine, or dragnet.

Scupper... channel through the boat's side to carry off water from the deck.

Shoals... submerged sandbanks.

Spar... a pole used as a mast, yard, boom or gaff.

Stanchion... an upright bar around the edge of the deck that supports the life line.

Starboard... the right side of the boat.

Stay... a rope supporting a spar or mast on a boat.

Staysail... a triangular sail similar to, but smaller than, the jib.

Stern... the rear of the boat.

Windlass... a hand winch for hauling or hoisting.

# Acknowledgements

Immeasurable gratitude to my family for your patience, invaluable assistance and encouragement during the rather long time it has taken me to write this book.

Special thanks go to:

To the excellent team at The Book Guild, who have guided me so well through my first experience of publishing.

Guy Reed for furnishing my book with his photography.

To Lynn McCombe for her plans of the deck areas of the *Helga Maria*.

To Gillian Herriot for her help with technicalities.

To Brian and Gill Farrow for their infectious enthusiasm for my book.

To my long-time special friend Stephanie for her never-failing encouragement and advice. Also to Farhad for taking the cover photo of me.

To Irene, Ian, Owen and Mac Wilson for listening as I read my story to them.

To Sheila and Gordon Wilson for looking after my dogs during my research absences from home.

And, not forgetting those two black Labradors, to Holly and Willow, for their companionship, lying by my side for hours as I've typed, and then, to clear my head, taken me out walking.

Thank you, friends, one and all.

# And Finally

I raise my glass to celebrate the memory of my skipper, Jack Lammiman, a seafarer and a gentleman. He and his boat, the *Helga Maria*, remain a legend in their home port of Whitby.

Where is she now?